Praise

Raising a Young Mo...

If a godly mom and dad could package themselves into a gift, it would open like the pages of Doreen and Karen's book. Their personal stories are uplifting and eye-opening, and their insight about the fruit of the Spirit will be as valuable to the parent as it is to the child. This is an easy read. The hard part will be deciding which tenderhearted, fun-filled, life-changing activity to do first. This will become a trusted resource for any parent who desires to raise a young modern-day princess in a perilous world.

CANDY ABBOTT
Executive Director, Mothers With a Mission

God is calling families to be intentional in raising their daughters. This new book by Karen and Doreen is a timely resource that will help educate and equip parents in raising godly girls in a world that can be confusing and distracting. *Raising a Young Modern-Day Princess* is built around practical applications drawn from biblical truths and the authors' personal experiences. Each chapter will surely inspire mothers and fathers to pursue their daughters in these busy and challenging times.

KRISTI TATRO
National Program Manager, American Heritage Girls

What a wonderful book! *Raising a Young Modern-Day Princess* is filled with practical ideas to energize your daughter's spiritual life. As you celebrate rites of passage in her life, you will create lifelong positive traditions and memories that will help infuse hope and faith. There are fresh ideas on every page.

JIM BURNS, PHD
President, HomeWord
Author of *Faith Conversations for Families* and *Confident Parenting*

In *Raising a Young Modern-Day Princess*, Doreen Hanna and Karen Whiting have penned a soon-to-be classic. This sweet and poignant book serves as a comprehensive step-by-step guide for raising a healthy, godly young woman. It captures the wholesome essence of what makes girls and young women so special. The Dad and Daughter Activities are a treasure and are worth the cost of the book alone. I highly recommend this for anyone raising a daughter.

RICK JOHNSON
Author of *Becoming the Dad Your Daughter Needs*

I've watched Doreen encourage, inspire, and empower girls to be aware of who they are, reach outside the box, increase their personal pride, and express the greatness they possess. We all need these enhancements to become and remain our very best. Young and all can reach the top with this insight.

PROFESSOR THELMA WELLS (MAMA T)
CEO, That A Girl Enrichment Tours

Packed with ideas, strategies, and activities, *Raising a Young Modern-Day Princess* can be your guide for raising your daughter as a beautiful princess in God's kingdom. Practical and insightful, this book will be a well-worn reference to return to with each parenting challenge you face.

KRISTEN KANSIEWICZ, LICENSED MENTAL HEALTH COUNSELOR

Author of *On Edge* and *Emotional Traps*

Teaching children to love and reflect Jesus in today's society challenges the best of parents. Thankfully resources such as *Raising a Young Modern-Day Princess* exist to make the task easier. This must-have book is a treasure trove of wisdom and practical ideas for parents desiring God's best for their little girls. I wish it had been available when my two daughters were young.

GRACE FOX

Author of *Tuck-Me-In Talks with Your Little Ones*

FOCUS FAMILY

PARENTING

RAISING A *Young* MODERN-DAY *Princess*

*Growing the Fruit of the Spirit
in Your Little Girl*

Doreen Hanna & Karen Whiting

*Tyndale House Publishers, Inc.
Carol Stream, Illinois*

Raising a Young Modern-Day Princess: Growing the Fruit of the Spirit in Your Little Girl

© 2016 Doreen Hanna and Karen Whiting

A Focus on the Family book published by Tyndale House Publishers, Inc., Carol Stream, Illinois 60188

Focus on the Family and the accompanying logo and design are federally registered trademarks of Focus on the Family, 8605 Explorer Drive, Colorado Springs, CO 80920.

TYNDALE and Tyndale's quill logo are registered trademarks of Tyndale House Publishers, Inc.

All Scripture quotations, unless otherwise marked, are taken from the *Holy Bible, New International Reader's Version*®, NIrV® Copyright © 1995, 1996, 1998 by Biblica, Inc.™ Used by permission of Zondervan. All rights reserved worldwide. (*www.zondervan.com*) The "NIrV" and "New International Reader's Version" are trademarks registered in the United States Patent and Trademark Office by Biblica, Inc.™

Scripture quotations marked (ESV) are from *The Holy Bible, English Standard Version*. Copyright © 2001 by CrosswayBibles, a publishing ministry of Good News Publishers. Used by permission. All rights reserved.

Scripture quotations marked (KJV) are taken from the *Holy Bible*, King James Version.

Scripture quotations marked (NASB) are taken from the *New American Standard Bible.*® Copyright © 1960, 1962, 1963, 1968, 1971, 1972, 1973, 1975, 1977, 1995 by The Lockman Foundation. Used by permission. (www.Lockman.org).

Scripture quotations marked (NIV) are taken from the *Holy Bible, New International Version*®, NIV®. Copyright © 1973, 1978, 1984 by Biblica, Inc.™ Used by permission of Zondervan. All rights reserved worldwide. (*www.zondervan.com*) The "NIV" and "New International Version" are trademarks registered in the United States Patent and Trademark Office by Biblica, Inc.™

Scripture quotations marked (TLB) are taken from *The Living Bible* [paraphrase], copyright © 1971. Used by permission of Tyndale House Publishers, Inc., Carol Stream, Illinois 60188. All rights reserved.

The use of material from or references to various websites does not imply endorsement of those sites in their entirety. Availability of websites and pages is subject to change without notice.

The authors are represented by Books & Such Literary Management, 52 Mission Circle, Suite 122, PMB 170, Santa Rosa, CA 95409-5370, booksandsuch.com.

Editor: Liz Duckworth

Cover design by Kristin Bakken

Cover photograph of ballerina copyright © Kristin Rogers Photography/Stocksy. All rights reserved.

Cover illustration of doodles copyright © blindspot/iStockphoto. All rights reserved.

Library of Congress Cataloging-in-Publication Data for this title can be found at www.loc.gov.

ISBN 978-1-58997-866-9

Printed in the United States of America

22	21	20	19	18	17	16
7	6	5	4	3	2	1

It is with the deepest gratitude that I dedicate this book to my mother, Ariel Quintana; Lucia Quintana, my late grandmother; and my wonderful friend and mentor, Emilie Horner. Each of you modeled characteristics of a good mother that as a young woman I desired to emulate.

Mom, you modeled faithfulness. My grandma Quintana demonstrated the wealth of kindness in her actions and words. Emilie, you still model today that the joy of the Lord is your strength. Each of you invested yourself into my life and guided me by your words and actions to believe in the person God created me to be, when I couldn't yet see it in myself. You equipped me to become a better woman and mom than I ever thought possible.

Brandy Corea and Kamy Hanna, I am delighted that God chose me to be your mother. My joy and gratitude has overflowed once again, because you both have so willingly given of your time and talents to further the vision God has given me. Thank you, my girls, for contributions that you have written or the stories that I have told about you in the contents of this book. I pray that those who peek into your lives through the words that are penned will be encouraged by your transparency that reveals your childhood frailty as well as your maturing strength and wisdom today.

Victory Ludwig, thank you for sharing your stories that revealed your vulnerability as a mom. Your pursuit of God's wisdom incorporated into your own life was clearly evident, as well as how you are imparting it into the lives of your children. Thank you for your contributions that will bring many moms great hope and encouragement.

Thank you, Larry Weeden, Pam Farrel, and Karen Whiting, for believing in the ministry of Modern Day Princess and coming alongside of me to see it published for many more eyes to see today's girls embracing their royalty as daughters of the King, true Modern-Day Princesses.

—DOREEN

To my young granddaughters, Princess Julia and Princess Lydia; my cousin, Princess Juliette; and my future granddaughters. This book is for your mom and each of you, so you will know you are a daughter of the King. Have fun together as you follow Jesus. May your life produce the wonderful fruit of the Spirit!

To my daughters Rebecca and Darlene. My journey with both of you has been wild, wonderful, and worthy! I'm thankful for the blessing of being your mother. May you enjoy being mothers as much as I do as you continue to be daughters of the King! Thanks for letting me share some of your stories of becoming true princesses.

In memory of my amazing husband, Jim, and my fantastic dad, John, who both treated me royally and lived out their faith as great examples.

Thank you, Doreen, for the vision for the book and desire to reach moms of young girls. May the Lord bless many girls and help them become daughters of the King through this ministry.

—KAREN

Contents

Foreword

"NANA!" Two excited, beautiful granddaughters rush toward me as I enter their home. They are decked head to toe in royal wear. Crowns adorn their long, lovely locks, and fancy jeweled shoes make a clickity-click-click sound as they hold up full chiffon skirts and bounce toward me with delight, showing off their majestic fashions. They are dressed as princesses today—and most days. But while their attire helps them pretend to be storybook princesses, there is a Book that has helped them act like true daughters of the King of Kings. Yes, my sweet granddaughters love the Bible and love living in a manner worthy of their calling (see Ephesians 4:1 and 2 Thessalonians 1:11, ESV).

It is for these two delightful princesses, and for young girls around the world, that I first agreed to team with my coauthor, Doreen Hanna, to write *Raising a Modern-Day Princess* and *Becoming a Modern-Day Princess Journal* for teen girls. Doreen has become a friend and a trusted voice on ways to proactively and creatively pour wisdom into the life of a young woman. In addition, Karen Whiting, the coauthor of this book, has penned many creative resources to help foster the life of a girl, including *The One Year My Princess Devotions*, a daily devotional my own granddaughters *love*. As I see the delight in their eyes, I am further motivated to look for ways to inspire them to live out the rich inheritance found in their identities as daughters of the King of Kings. This book will help them do that, just as it will help you inspire your own daughter to fully comprehend, then live out, her divine destiny.

Because I raised three sons and worked in youth ministry, I saw how difficult life could be for young women who might be all *vogue* on the outside but *vague* on the inside. I longed to help girls and women grasp their upward call in Christ. So I have spent a lifetime writing, speaking, leading, and mentoring hundreds of girls, young women, and moms. I am also the mother-in-law to three amazing, godly women, and I have seen firsthand the work and wisdom that need to be poured into a girl's life in order for her to become a truly beautiful, godly, loving, servant-hearted princess, a daughter of the King of all Kings—God!

From the moment our Modern-Day Princess books for teenage girls were released by Focus on the Family/Tyndale House Publishers, mothers and fathers of little girls—even expectant moms—wanted a book that would help guide a young girl in godliness as she grows. In *Raising a Young Modern-Day Princess*, Karen Whiting and Doreen Hanna have created a masterful interactive experience between parents and their young daughter. These two experienced moms and leaders have penned a resource to weave critical character into the life of a young lady.

In *10 Questions Kids Ask About Sex*, we share a key question we asked in our home. We have a family motto, "Those who honor God, God honors" (see 1 Samuel 2:30), so we taught our kids to check in with their inner GPS before they said or did anything by asking themselves, Does this show honor for:

God?
People?
Self?

It is a simple sentence with profound and lasting results. *Raising a Young Modern-Day Princess* has a similar goal of weaving the traits of a princess into the life of a younger girl in a natural, yet life-changing, way. The goal of the book you hold will help you pass on the value of being a PRINCESS who is:

Prayerful
Respectful
Inspired
Noble
Compassionate
Encourager
Self-controlled
Servant

These are virtuous traits that will ensure future victories in your little girl's life! This book will prepare your little princess now for the next step of a rite of passage, which can happen when she becomes a teenager. Then you'll be able to use the tools in the book *Raising a Modern-Day Princess*. For now, you can plan special tea parties to help her learn manners and etiquette to accompany the character and inner values that become a little princess. She will reflect back on these tea parties and life lessons in years to come. Each inter-action and every celebration helps you engage your daughter in conversations and connections to glean wisdom from you and from the God who created her. This treasure trove will serve her well on the path ahead.

In *Raising a Modern-Day Princess*, I shared that my husband and I had the goal of leaving a "trademark" on our children with Traditions and Memories. Traditions are those things you do year in and out, day in and day out, that layer in your values. The activities in this book include many precious traditions.

Memories are those "once in a lifetime" or occasional special events that become markers of celebration, or a way to honor your daughter as she progresses on her journey of virtue. This book includes ideas for special tea parties and other creative activities that you can use to celebrate your daughter's development.

As a family, once a year we have a "Learner and Leader Who Loves God Day," when we negotiate privileges and responsibilities for the year for each child. We choose a trait for the year and a verse for the year to pray over each child. We also give each one a gift to acknowledge the godly leader he or she is becoming. That gift is three things: *personal* (something personally selected so the child knows we were thinking of him or her as an individual); *practical* (something we would buy anyway, so it doesn't break the bank); and *prophetic* (something that speaks to the promise, potential, or passionate calling we see God developing in that child). In doing this, year after year, our children gained the critical inner character needed to grow up and become the godly leaders they are today.

I see these same wonderful qualities in the book you are

holding right now. *Raising a Young Modern-Day Princess* is *practical.* It's written to help your young daughter grow into a godly woman through the many activities and bite-sized biblical teachings included here. This book is also *personal.* You will be able to select activities and create quality time with your little princess, enhancing and enriching your relationship with her. After sowing the seeds of a strong relationship with you today, she will naturally long to keep that strong relationship with you—and God—in the days ahead. Finally, this book is also *prophetic.* It will help you get to know your daughter and see how God uniquely designed her. By cooperating with the way God wired her, you will see the fruit of this verse in her life: "Train up a child in the way he should go; even when he is old he will not depart from it" (Proverbs 22:6, ESV).

By implementing the ideas and activities in *Raising a Young Modern-Day Princess,* you will learn her personality, motivations, and talents. In addition, you will give her the vital skills to daily *be* a Modern-Day Princess now and in the future. Most importantly, you will be passing on those timeless and eternal values and beliefs to help her handle life in this ever-changing world. In a word, you are handing her the ability to *succeed.*

So turn the page, and enjoy your journey as you walk next to your little princess. You will love the joy of watching her grow into a lovely young lady, with courage, confidence, and creativity to become all God designed her to be.

Pam Farrel

Pam is the author or coauthor of 40 books,
including *Men Are like Waffles—Women Are like
Spaghetti, Raising a Modern-Day Princess,*
and *Becoming a Modern-Day Princess Journal.*

Introduction

As a mother, you have special dreams for your daughter or daughters. Do you remember when you first held your precious baby girl, with a heart full of hope and joy? What did you envision for that little bundle wrapped in pink?

Since that day, you just might have discovered that the path to raising a daughter of the King is less than straight and easy. The world we live in today constantly throws out challenges and obstacles to bringing up a future woman of God—one who is beautiful inside and out.

But rest assured, you have guides along the way who are ready to share valuable tools for understanding and nurturing a girl. This journey is designed to equip you to bring forth the fruit of the Spirit in your daughter, inspiring her to become a princess with purpose, character, and strength.

So let's start with a look at how it all began—and God's calling to a ministry that makes an eternal difference for moms and their daughters.

A Mother's Dream

For more than a decade, I (Doreen) have served as president of a ministry that is all about princesses—Treasured

Celebrations. Through the years, I've seen how mothers want their daughter(s) to embrace the beautiful traits and truths of a real princess, not a fairy-tale princess. Launching a ministry about God's best for our precious daughters started with a simple phone call.

In March 1999, a local church asked me to speak at its mother/daughter banquet on the topic "Celebrate! You're a Daughter of the King." The underlying message was supposed to focus on older women mentoring young girls.

I said yes, but as I hung up the phone, I wondered, *What does it really mean to be a daughter of the King?* I knew it was a biblical concept, but I had to figure out what that idea looked like in our modern churches and society. Within seconds the answer came to me: *A daughter of the King is a princess!*

My research into the topic took me on an amazing journey of discovery. I came across a book for Jewish parents who were preparing a bat mitzvah for their daughters. Then I read a book for twelve-year-old Jewish girls going through their rites of passage into young womanhood when turning thirteen. I found that parents committed their daughters to mentors who came alongside them weekly for a full year, preparing each girl to celebrate her step into womanhood. First a girl's mentor reinforced the parents' and her synagogue's teaching. Then her etiquette was refined and improved. Every effort was made to provide the girl with a sense of purpose, value, and strength as she grew into womanhood. At the conclusion of this important year, a girl would receive her father's blessing.

Through God's leading, my research into bat mitzvahs enabled me to share ideas for preparing girls for womanhood with mentors and moms at that banquet in 1999. Yet I walked away from the event with a question left in my heart: "What rites of passage do Christian girls have today in our churches?" I knew of nothing at that time.

Researching further, I learned about debutante balls for girls in certain society groups. And I discovered some denominational churches had teen groups called "Daughters of the King" that provided biblical training about becoming a young woman.

Still, I couldn't find a celebration where a girl's father imparted the blessing. So I knew the Lord was calling me to write.

Soon I was working on my first rite-of-passage curriculum with the assistance of my two daughters. Brandy Corea, my lovely eldest daughter, has been married for twenty years to her husband, Roberto, and they are the parents of our four grandchildren: Kevin, Shekinah, Hannah, and Josiah. Kamy Hanna, my beautiful single daughter, is two years younger than Brandy. She has been my right hand in this ministry throughout the years. And she cheered me on when Focus on the Family embraced my book proposal and published *Raising a Modern-Day Princess* in 2010.

After fifteen years, our program has been implemented in every state in the nation and in twenty-two countries across the world. I am continually in awe of God's favor every time I write or speak of it today.

Over the years, I've often been asked, "What do you have for moms of little girls?" Thus Karen and I started on a new journey for younger daughters and the parents who love them.

Some moms have said, "I never had this opportunity, but I would love for my daughter to experience this type of mentoring." It's not too late for you, Mom! It can start now as you teach your daughter. You will be the best example for your daughter as she sees your teachable spirit and willingness to learn right beside her! It is never too late to embrace your own royal status as a daughter of the King and to enjoy the benefits of kingdom living—beginning with a Christ-focused life.

Some moms already live as daughters of the King. Therefore, we hope to provide you with fresh perspectives and creative activities enabling you and your daughter(s) to apply what is presented within each chapter, equipping girls to carry on a royal family legacy.

A Mother's Heart

As a mother, a grandmother, and an author of several books for girls and women, I (Karen) am thrilled to share my experiences and knowledge to help raise the next generation of daughters of God the King. I have five children; two are girls. Rebecca is my first child and Darlene is my fourth. You'll be meeting them in some of the stories in this book. I discovered the heart of a mother first in my mother and grandmothers, who always had time for me and created fun activities for us to share.

As a young girl I enjoyed tea parties with my maternal grandmother and a mother who treated me as a princess while giving me lessons on etiquette and life skills. In turn, I held tea parties with my daughters as part of their training to be princesses of the kingdom. Now I enjoy holding tea parties for young girls at churches and schools.

I grew up in a small community with many relatives, including lots of cousins who lived only a few houses away. Because I was the oldest girl in my generation, my grandmothers encouraged me to show my cousins how to be a lady, leading by example. As a Christian, I also wanted to pass on the joy of knowing Jesus. I created activities that combined fun, faith, and values for my cousins and, later, for my children and their friends.

As my children grew, people encouraged me to tell my stories of parenting my girls and the activities I developed. It's been my pleasure to reminisce and share ideas to bring up a new generation of girls who will embrace Christ and develop the inner beauty of lasting values, by nurturing the fruit of the Spirit.

When I first embraced each of my precious daughters, I felt a surge of joy and quickly planted dreams for each of them within my heart. I wanted my daughters to become beautiful women inside and out, and to make good choices. But I've realized that we mothers don't control what our daughters will become. The fruit of the Spirit is produced by planting the right seeds, nurturing the growth through watering, weeding, and fertilizing, then trusting the Holy Spirit ultimately to bring forth desired results.

Girls envision a princess as one who is loved, cherished, and surrounded by beauty. But being a real princess in God's family goes much deeper than surface beauty. In this book, you'll discover how a parent can develop a daughter's inner beauty and character, as well as showing her the unconditional love of the King.

I am still close to my two lovely daughters and want to share ideas with moms so they can nurture their daughters' growth. As a creative person I often developed my own activities to nurture my daughters' character development and faith. I've incorporated many of these in the activity section of each chapter. These activities nurtured the fruits of the Spirit in my daughters and built strong mother-daughter bonds. I hope you will also build memories and lasting bonds with your daughter(s) as you enjoy implementing the activities.

Themes to Discover

Several themes are woven into the pages of this book to bring more depth to the parent-child relationship and to provide engaging activities to develop the fruit of the Spirit. Here's a preview of what you'll find!

La Belle Jardinière

Jesus used the analogy of a tree and its fruit numerous times. He said, "The tree is known by its fruit" (Matthew 12:33, NASB). He told the parable of a gardener asking for another season to fertilize and care for a tree that did not bear good fruit (see Luke 13:6-9). Those images from Jesus' teaching inspired us to plant and nurture growth in our daughters in such a way as to produce the fruit of the Spirit.

The gardener is one who tends the plants. In the famous French painting *La Belle Jardinière* by Renaissance artist Raphael, motherhood is symbolized as a beautiful gardener.

As mothers we are gardeners, and, we hope, ones with beautiful hearts, as the French words for "beautiful gardener" imply. Each chapter in *Raising a Young Modern-Day Princess* begins with a thought about you, Mom, La Belle Jardinière who is nurturing the fruit of the Spirit daily in the heart of your daughter.

Proverbs 17:22 tells us that "a cheerful heart is good medicine" (NIV). As parents, we strive to do everything right so our children will become well-adjusted, respectable individuals. But in the midst of our focused parenting efforts, they sometimes surprise us with moments of innocent, unexpected humor that bring a smile or even a hearty laugh. To tickle your funny bone, we have also seasoned each chapter with a cute quote from and about today's kids.

Daughters of the King

"As many as received Him, to them He gave the right to become children of God, even to those who believe in His name" (John 1:12, NASB).

God calls us all to believe in Him. In turn, He blesses believers and welcomes each one as His child. Thus, we are daughters of the King. In the Lord's Prayer, we pray, "Thy kingdom come," a reminder of our eternal place with God in heaven. Throughout this book we'll use the term *princess*, and by that we mean "child of God."

Dad's Toolbox and Special Activities

Each chapter includes sidebar ideas for dads, or step-in-dads, as we like to call them (such as a grandpa, uncle, or good family friend who connects with your daughter). Little girls look to their dads or other males for approval and love. Our prayer is that if a girl's birth father is unavailable, then a step-in-dad will become part of her life. God is calling many men to become "fathers to the fatherless." He promises to bless those who help children who need someone to fulfill the caring role of a loving father (see Deuteronomy 24:19-21).

Fatherhood is a rite of passage, a new season of a man's life. It will be one of the most rewarding journeys and, at times, one of the most challenging. I (Doreen) hope to provide you dads with some essential tools that my father (a carpenter by trade) and my husband, Chad (a seasoned home and hotel contractor), both used. I will compare the tools to fatherhood skills, to show how to build, fix, or refine your daughter's life. Picture yourself as you mentally lay out a blueprint and collect some of the most important tools required for the task, placing them in your toolbox to use as you help your daughter see the attributes of a loving dad.

In each chapter I (Karen) included ideas for dads to connect with their daughters and activities just for your little princess and you, the special man in her life.

Treasures

We want our daughters to treasure God and to understand how much He treasures them. We speak of treasures and use a treasure-box activity that connects Bible stories with special items to store in the treasure box.

We also know God treasures our daughters and we are all precious to Him. Let the treasure box be a special connection for your daughter and her relationship to God.

Personalities

According to Psalm 139:14, God skillfully makes each individual. Along with outward features such as eye color and nose shape, God also creates each one's innermost being. That includes personality. Research, including studies at the University of Edinburgh and the Albert Einstein College of Medicine, continues to show a connection between a person's genetic makeup and his or her personality.

In chapter 1, different personalities are described, and two simple personality profiles are provided to help identify your personality and your daughter's personality. Each chapter provides ideas on how to nurture a particular fruit of the Spirit through your daughter's personality strengths.

Fruit of the Spirit

Fruit is the natural outcome when a fruit-bearing tree or bush grows and receives necessary water, nutrients, and care. We cannot simply wish that our daughters will be kind, joyful, or loving, or demonstrate other attributes of the fruit of the Spirit. For real fruit to be produced in a person's life, the seeds must be planted and nurtured. Think of it like this: We can plant a watermelon seed, but only God can provide the sunshine!

As we journey together through the chapters of this book, we'll explore ways to nurture fruitful virtues in our daughters. At the same time, let's remember to trust the outcome to our heavenly Father. As we help our daughters grow to be like Christ, those fruits, or character traits, will also grow as He develops them in His image.

Princess Mothering Chart

To show the relationship between your efforts and the desired outcome in your daughter's life, we created a chart that also reflects this book's layout. Each mother's action is listed in the form of an acrostic and serves as a key to nurturing a particular princess attribute to help develop a specific fruit.

Each chapter begins with the mother's action and progresses to show you how to nurture the desired trait and fruits in your daughter's life. Each chapter ends with a variety of activities to practice and to apply these ideas and principles. You'll also find tools to help develop your own skills as a mother of a princess.

The chart shows how your actions as a mom can lead to princess attributes, then to specific fruits.

Mother's actions	Princess attributes	Resulting fruit
P-erceive	**P**-rayerful	*Faithfulness*
R-efine	**R**-espectful	*Peace*
I-nspire	**I**-nspired	*Joy*
N-urture	**N**-oble	*Goodness*
C-ultivate	**C**-ompassionate	*Gentleness*
E-ncourage	**E**-ncourager	*Kindness*
S-how Her	**S**-elf-controlled	*Patience and self-control*
S-erve	**S**-ervant	*Love*

The last chapter includes two important celebrations. First, there's a tea party book launch to enjoy before starting the book. (Be sure to flip to the back to see those plans and ideas.) Then, there's a blessing ceremony to hold after the book is completed. You're encouraged to plan and complete these activities to get the most out of this book.

Our Desire for Moms

You might want to commit Galatians 5:22-23 to memory, because it forms the foundation for your journey with your daughter through this book. "When the Holy Spirit controls our lives he will produce this kind of fruit in us: love, joy, peace, patience, kindness, goodness, faithfulness, gentleness and self-control; and here there is no conflict with Jewish laws" (TLB).

It's important to note that the fruit of the Spirit grows out of a heart that trusts in Jesus Christ. When a young girl comes to know Jesus personally, she can be confident that she is a daughter of the King, one who lives as a true princess. We pray that all moms and their daughters will ultimately embrace their royalty and use the keys of the kingdom that will open doors to experience God's blessings. May you see the fruit of the Spirit in your own life and your daughter(s)—the evidence of both young and mature Modern-Day Princesses.

Leading a Child to Christ

If you are looking for a helpful way to introduce your daughter to Jesus, here is a simple approach, adapted from *FaithLaunch: A Simple Plan to Ignite Your Child's Love for Jesus* by John Trent, PhD, and Jane Vogel:

Start your conversation by saying something like: "I like being with you. God likes being with you, too. He even wants us to come live with Him forever someday."

Open your Bible to 1 John 3:1 and read it aloud.

Say, "God wants us to be part of His family! Because of Jesus, we can be God's children. Do you know what Jesus did that made it possible to be God's children?"

After your daughter responds, confirm or clarify her answer by reading 1 John 2:12.

For older children, ages eight and up, you can use the word *relationship*. Ask your daughter what kind of relationship she likes to have with a friend, with you, and with a sibling. What kind of relationship would she like to have with God?

Help her understand the kind of relationship God would like to have with her by looking at John 14:23-27 and John 15:14-16.

Explain to her that God invites us to join His family by believing in His Son, Jesus.

If your daughter hasn't responded to that invitation yet, ask whether she would like to do so now. If the answer is yes, you may want to lead her in a prayer like this:

Dear God,

I know that my life isn't right without You. I know that I sin—I do things that are wrong, and don't do things I should. You said You love me even though I'm still a sinner. Will You please forgive me and give me a new start?

I want You to be my heavenly Father. I believe Your Son, Jesus, died to pay the price for my sin and rose to life again. I accept Him as my Savior to rescue me, and as my Lord to be in charge of my life.

In Jesus' name I pray. Amen.

If your daughter isn't ready, don't press the matter. You may want to pray with her, though, asking God to help her to discover the treasure of getting to know the One who loves us so much.

1

Guiding and Growing
a Daughter of the King

*La Belle Jardinière dreams of a fruitful garden filled
with beauty and begins planning for the future.*

Guiding Mothers
Princess Attribute—Teachable Spirit
Introduction to the Fruit of the Spirit

THE MORE YOU understand your child and her needs, the easier it will be to guide her. We are here to help you learn as much as you can about the way God has uniquely designed your little girl. So this chapter focuses on personality types, using a simple profile that enables you to identify your daughter's personality.

The activities at the end of the chapter will also help you introduce the fruit of the Spirit to your daughter and provide ideas about nurturing her according to her individual personality.

And because Dad plays such a vital role in raising his princess, it's important to remind him to focus on his daughter's individuality to help her grow. Karen's cousin Gary learned how much his young daughter valued individual time with him when they went on their first daddy-daughter "date."

Gary's Story: A Butterfly Tea Party

Mary helped her three-year-old daughter, Juliette, prepare for a special day with her dad, Gary. Then Mary left for an outing with their son, leaving everything up to Gary. It took him a little while to get the hang of this first date with his daughter.

Before they even left, Juliette spun around and around. She kept telling her daddy she was ready to leave. Then she beamed as she looked up at him and said, "I have a new dress."

Gary realized his little girl wanted a compliment. He squatted down, looked into her eyes, and said, "Juliette, you look beautiful." He took her hand and they walked to the car. After buckling up and pulling out of the driveway, Gary thought, *I think I'll just turn on the radio and listen to the basketball championship.* But then he heard his daughter's voice.

"Today is a Daddy day. I'm so happy."

Uh-oh, Gary thought, *I'd better listen for a while. It's an hour's drive, so she'll quiet down soon.* But Juliette chattered on happily and asked questions throughout the whole ride. Every time Gary thought about asking her to be quiet, she repeated that it was a Daddy day. He sighed, realizing he wouldn't be hearing the game, and stayed tuned in to her.

At a nature center they headed to the butterfly garden and tea party. Gary discovered he was expected to help Juliette make a butterfly crown, take a nature walk, dance with her, participate in other activities, then sit and have tea. He cheerfully helped his little girl and chatted with her.

He helped twist chenille stem antennae and complimented Juliette when she donned her butterfly crown. He noticed her polite manners and praised her. They laughed together as they sipped their drinks and ate their tiny cakes.

Juliette smiled the entire afternoon and chatted with the other little girls and the leaders. On the drive home she fell fast asleep. As he thought about their day, Gary realized he'd seen a new side of his daughter. *She's a little social butterfly,* he thought.

Gary looked forward to more dates with Juliette and special bonding times. He knew his role was to teach her how to expect a gentleman to behave and prepare her to make good choices as she grew up. And he was grateful for the opportunity to help shape his daughter's life and her future.

How to Be a Guiding Mom

Effective parenting includes responding to your daughter as Gary did by listening to Juliette's words and understanding her unique bent. You can tune in to your child's personality, whether she is bubbly and outgoing, quiet and reserved, relaxed or energetic. Sometimes a gift will come your way to help you discover more or receive deeper insights. A personality profile is one of those gifts we believe will help you effectively guide your daughter.

I (Doreen) have learned from personality profiles that both Karen's cousin Juliette and my daughter Hannah are Social Butterflies. Hannah loves to talk and tell stories, for example. She is ready to give a cheerful, uplifting word or hug when needed. She's in tune with others and makes an effort to reach out and pray when she sees someone is hurting. While some of her Social Butterfly characteristics are obvious on the surface, it's also helpful to use a personality profile to clearly identify her unique needs and gifts.

When it comes to raising a little princess, you may have encountered some distinctive traits that generally apply to females. Of course, children differ widely, but you might observe that some of these behaviors are more common with very young daughters compared to sons:

- They are most likely little chatterboxes and enjoy having an audience, even if it's an audience of one.
- They tend to gesture more, starting young by waving bye-bye.
- Hand movements reveal their desire to communicate, even without words.
- Girls are quicker to pay attention to other people's facial expressions, making them prone to be more empathetic to others in distress.

Characteristics that come into play within a few months of life demonstrate each girl's own little personality.

In recent years I've come to appreciate the value of identifying your own personality traits, as well as those of your child. This truly helps us understand how uniquely God made each of us, and it also gives us new ideas about the best ways to motivate individual children.

Personality profiling has changed the lives of adults, including myself. Thousands of people have gained insights about themselves and others by using the *Wired That Way*

Personality Profile written by Marita and Florence Littauer, personality experts for more than thirty-five years.

Like most parents, I began parenting my little girls without a personality profile. But it would have been so helpful to have had one during their formative years. By God's grace, a mom's intuition, and observing my daughters' behavior, I was able to assess some of their basic personality traits. When I was introduced to the Personality Profile, I took it immediately and began to discover what God had placed within me. I am a Social Butterfly and Born Leader, in that order.

Understanding myself helped me to be a better mom to my girls. I recognized my weaknesses as well as my strengths and saw how they influenced and affected my daughters. Then, discovering their personalities as they began to develop equipped me to encourage and to guide them individually. As a result, they were able to better understand and comprehend my instructions or requests, and to respond appropriately.

A Social Butterfly is just one of four personalities. The others are: Born Leader, Princess of Order, and Everyone's Friend. The four basic personality profiles can help you quickly identify some of the unique, God-given characteristics of your daughter, her siblings, and friends. The mom's profile is more detailed; it will enable you to recognize the personality traits God chose to place within you. It's also a great tool to begin understanding other family members and people in your life.

At the end of this chapter, you'll find two simple personality profiles to help evaluate your own and your daughter's personality. I trust they will provide insights to help strengthen your relationship with your daughter. Take time to complete both profiles, and you'll see how relevant they are to the material in this book.

Many years ago I identified my daughter Brandy as my Born Leader. As soon as she began to talk, she lined up her dolls and told them what to do and how to do it. She sounded just like me! The tone of her voice sounded more commanding than encouraging. I took note and worked to change my way of leading her, encouraging her to follow rather than always just instructing.

Kamy is our Social Butterfly. The day she finally began to talk, she spoke in full sentences. From then on she talked incessantly. She loved making others laugh. Learning to listen and obey was her greatest challenge. Knowing my girls' personalities was a tremendous help: Brandy felt safe when all was in order. Fun motivated Kamy to get things done! I remember watching Brandy begin to understand her sister. She would say, "Come on, Kam, let's do this. It will be fun!" Kamy learned to talk Brandy into a chore by saying, "Bran, let's do this together, and it will get done quicker!"

Understanding yourself and each other will produce greater peace in your homes.

Developing Your Daughter's Teachable Spirit

We are both certified personality trainers and have spent years studying and working with different personalities. I (Karen) also noticed great differences in my two daughters' personalities. Those differences brought out the best in them—and the worst when they clashed! They both loved being around people, but Rebecca, the Born Leader, wanted control and wanted to lead everyone. I started to discover Rebecca's personality while she developed in the womb. My Born Leader decided to dictate when I could sit and kicked hard if I rested when she evidently wanted me to walk or work. She seemed to set goals that included swimming twenty laps around the pool in the womb every night before she settled down so I could sleep.

Darlene, a combination of Social Butterfly and Everyone's Friend, cared more about turning any activity into a party, being the center of attention, and keeping peace. In restaurants, Rebecca cringed when Darlene stood up to dance around and spoke to strangers at other tables. Darlene pouted if Rebecca scolded or prompted her to sit down. I often reminded them they were different and needed to rejoice in the uniqueness of the other. Most of the time they liked to play and pray together, with Rebecca leading and Darlene joyfully joining in the plans.

Let's look at the four personality types. A Social Butterfly, also known as a popular *sanguine*, loves attention and fun and always seems full of energy. These girls are exuberant, like bright colors, and make friends instantly.

A Born Leader, who is also called a powerful *choleric*, wants control and is a natural leader. These girls are goal oriented and accomplish more than any other personality. They desire loyalty, respect, and appreciation for their work. No challenge is too great for these little princesses.

A Princess of Order, also known as a *melancholy*, likes to think and is happy to play alone. She is quiet, thoughtful, and hesitant to try something until she believes she can do it perfectly. She can whine and complain a lot, but she also stays focused on her task.

Everyone's Friend, also called a *phlegmatic*, is a content child who likes to rest and resists change. This child is naturally witty and very likable and seeks peace. These girls tend to procrastinate and seldom worry.

When you complete the personality profiles at the end of this chapter, you might see your daughter in a new light, and better understand what brings her joy and what challenges her. Working with your little girl's natural God-given wiring will make a huge difference in the way you relate together. And understanding your own personality might help you see more clearly why you sometimes don't see eye to eye, or why you share some traits (for better or worse!).

Fruitful Activities

Fruit of the Spirit Verse

"When the Holy Spirit controls our lives he will produce this kind of fruit in us: love, joy, peace, patience, kindness, goodness, faithfulness, gentleness and self-control; and here there is no conflict with Jewish laws" (Galatians 5:22-23, TLB).

Fruit Salad

Make a fruit salad with your daughter. Enjoy eating it, and talk about how you'll be discovering a special kind of "fruit" that will grow in her heart and character. Talk about the different spiritual fruits in the verse. Explain that you'll have fun doing activities that develop those fruits so that your daughter can become a true daughter of the King.

Shop for Fruit

Take your daughter to a farmer's market, or check the produce aisle at your local grocery store. Talk about fruits that are ripe and ones that are spoiled or not yet ripe. Explain that bananas may need more time to ripen, or that a watermelon might need a thump to determine if it is ripe. Talk about how fruits give us lots of nutrients and help us grow. Chat about how the fruit of the Spirit helps us and allows us to bring good things to the lives of others.

Helping Daughters Understand Personalities

Help your daughter understand her unique personality combination and that of her friends.

- Read a copy of *The Treasure Tree: Helping Kids Understand Their Personality* (by John and Cindy Trent and Gary and Norma Smalley) and talk about personalities.

- Read Winnie-the-Pooh stories and princess stories, and chat about the characters' personalities. Who likes to be the leader? Who likes to party? Who is quieter? Who likes to sit and eat?

Obstacle Course and a Teachable Spirit

Set up a short obstacle course. Include or create the following (or vary it depending on what you have around the house):

- chairs to go around or under
- blocks to jump over

- a tunnel to crawl through
- a wood beam to walk across
- a ball to bounce or roll or drop into a bucket

After your daughter goes through the obstacle course, talk about the experience. Ask what she went over or under, and what she had to remember to do. Maybe she had to bend, turn, twist, do things in order. Or maybe she had to redo something like picking up a dropped ball and trying to toss it through a hoop again. Affirm the way she met the challenges.

Talk about the challenges of becoming a true daughter of the King. Point out that growing the fruit of the Spirit can be challenging too. We might forget to be kind and push someone in anger. We might want our way and not be self-controlled enough to wait our turn. Encourage her that the process usually will be fun and that she will be able to succeed with God's help. Be willing to see challenges as adventures. That's being teachable!

Dad and Daughter Activities

Prepare to Raise a Princess Commitment

Look at your precious daughter. Choose to make a written commitment in her baby book or letter to her. Keep a copy in your wallet or post it somewhere you will see it often.

Promise her:

- I will value you all the days of your life.
- I will invest time in your days.

- I will believe in your dreams.

- I will guard your purity and your heart.

- I will correct and guide you as needed.

- I will love and treasure you always.

Dad and Daughter Dates

Schedule some time for your little girl to go on a date with you. It might be a walk or a short trip for ice cream. Let it be a special time to be together. Remember to:

- Listen to your daughter.

- Compliment her.

- Be a gentleman.

- Thank her at the end of the date.

Ideas for Daddy dates don't have to be complicated or expensive. Here are some possibilities to get you started:

- Make a snack together.

- Watch a movie.

- Read to her.

- Do science experiments.

- Check the car together and wash it.

- Check a bike or tricycle together.

- Use a phone or camera for "photo ops," either inside or outside.

- Let her sing to you. (Sing together too.)

- Have a tea party.

- Share a little "beauty time." Can you braid her hair or tie a ribbon in it?

- Go on a shopping spree to a garage sale or dollar store.

- Pass a ball.

- Dance.

- Dress up Dad.

- Make something (from wood or even cardboard, such as a princess crown bedroom door sign).

- Build a fort with blankets and a table, or even a tree fort.

- Play miniature golf.

- Fly a kite.

- Go to the beach or a pool.

Mom's Tools

Encourage a Teachable Attitude

Rejoice when your princess learns something new. When your princess fails, encourage her to try again. Remind her that past practice can be turned into success.

- Praise your child for effort and not just results.

- Share stories of trying harder, like *The Little Engine That Could.*

- Show your daughter a task, and do it with her until she masters it. Let her do more of the work each time. For example: Make a bed. Show her how to do it one day, then have her help with some of the steps each day until she can do it by herself.

- Don't scold failures. Explain what is incorrect and how to do better next time.

- Accept a child's ability and a child's results.

- Brainstorm ideas for learning something that seems hard.

- Make a picture book of steps, including failures, showing your daughter mastering a skill or task.

Mom's Personality Profile Directions

Read each statement across each row. In box 1, 2, 3, or 4 place an X under the one that most often applies to you in that row. Total the X's at the bottom of each column. You should have two columns with higher numbers than the other two that identify your dominant personalities. Most often you will be a combination of two types.

1	2	3	4
☐ I am enthusiastic; I love to talk and to tell stories.	☐ I am outspoken and confidently share my opinion when asked.	☐ I approach new people cautiously and am very sensitive to their feelings.	☐ In a new situation, I would rather listen than talk.
☐ I tend to make quick decisions.	☐ The decisions I make are usually right.	☐ The decisions I make are based on all the facts.	☐ I don't like making decisions— others can.
☐ I make friends easily; I'm seen as cheerful and bubbly.	☐ I like to lead and organize the group.	☐ I am very loyal to my friends, but I enjoy being alone, too.	☐ I am easygoing and relaxed in a group, and I have a dry sense of humor when you know me better.
☐ I love to volunteer and inspire others to join in.	☐ I thrive on challenge and success.	☐ I have very high standards, and I love the details involved in work.	☐ I'm a good mediator, and I can find the easiest way to accomplish a task.

1	2	3	4
☐ I'm often perceived as silly or wide-eyed and innocent.	☐ I'm often perceived as controlling and competitive.	☐ I'm often perceived as a perfectionist and a loner.	☐ I'm often perceived as low-key or indecisive.
☐ Life should be fun and exciting!	☐ Life should be productive and adventurous!	☐ Life should be beautiful and meaningful!	☐ Life should be relaxed and comfortable!
☐ I get bored easily.	☐ I hate mistakes.	☐ I need my space.	☐ I tend to compromise.
☐ I live joyfully and in the moment.	☐ I live fearlessly and independently.	☐ I live thoughtfully and sincerely.	☐ I live contentedly and at peace.
☐ If I were stranded on an island . . . I'd find other people to befriend.	☐ If I were stranded on an island . . . I'd figure out how toget us rescued.	☐ If I were stranded on an island . . . I'd explore and document its beauty.	☐ If I were stranded on an island . . . I'd relax and enjoy the beach.
Total _____	**Total** _____	**Total** _____	**Total** _____

Directions for Little Girl's Personality Profile

Read each statement, then check the one in each row across that most often applies to your little girl. Total at the bottom of each column.

Note: It is most common to see a check here or there in other columns. That is not unusual. However, you will see your daughter most likely scoring highest in one of the columns that identify her dominant personality.

Social Butterfly	Born Leader	Princess of Order	Everyone's Friend
Strengths	**Strengths**	**Strengths**	**Strengths**
☐ loves to tell her story	☐ tends to be more serious	☐ more sensitive and thoughtful	☐ has a quiet nature
☐ too quick to make a decision	☐ likes being the leader	☐ content to be alone	☐ naturally kind to others
☐ likes being the center of attention	☐ tends to always take charge	☐ happy in smaller groups	☐ very easygoing
☐ likes to talk rather than listen	☐ likes order	☐ appreciates pretty things	☐ great listener
☐ makes friends easily	☐ naturally confident	☐ likes order	☐ content to watch the group play
☐ loves excitement	☐ self-sufficient	☐ prone to love art or music	☐ is a peacemaker
Total _____	**Total** _____	**Total** _____	**Total** _____

Things to work on	Things to work on	Things to work on	Things to work on
☐ Forgetfulness	☐ too controlling	☐ easily saddened	☐ Stubbornness
☐ tends to exaggerate	☐ impatient	☐ wants everything perfect	☐ compromises too easily
☐ never likes to be serious	☐ prone to be self-centered	☐ anxious over small details	☐ hates too much noise
☐ tends to be naive	☐ can be obsessive	☐ doesn't like change	☐ must feel valued
☐ Disorganized	☐ insensitive to others	☐ can get overstimulated	☐ greater need for emotional support
☐ leaves things unfinished	☐ bossy	☐ oversensitive	☐ always finds the easy way out
Total _____	**Total** _____	**Total** _____	**Total** _____

You can learn a lot more about personality profiles and how they affect your parenting by reading the book *Personality Plus for Parents: Understanding What Makes Your Child Tick* by Florence Littauer.

Dad's Toolbox

A blueprint is a plan that influences the subsequent design of a project. Isn't that what you desire to do for your daughter? You want to create a biblical plan that will be beautifully designed for her, and you want her to follow that plan to help her live life well.

An architect's blueprint is admired for its clean lines and fine details, providing vision and direction. The carpenter or contractor studies the blueprint, then fills his box with the necessary tools to begin and ultimately complete the project.

Look for Dad's Toolbox in each chapter to discover insights about using the appropriate tool to build purpose, value, and strength in your little girl's life. I (Doreen) am happy to share these tools based on observations about my own father, who was a carpenter, and my husband, Chad, a home and hotel contractor.

I am going to look for a frog in the backyard to kiss. Only I don't want it to turn into a prince. I want to turn into a frog.

LAYLA, huffingtonpost.com

The Fruit of Faithfulness in Your Princess's Life

*La Belle Jardinière tests the soil to identify its properties,
then knows how to work and enrich the soil to make it
more fertile for producing the best fruits.*

Perceptive Mothers
Princess Attribute—Prayerful
Fruit of the Spirit—Faithfulness

PERCEPTIVE MOTHERING IS a gift given by God to moms. In the same way that a gardener tests the soil before enriching it, the gift of perception helps a mother discover how to best nurture her daughter based on her child's needs.

The gift of being a perceptive mom can also enable her to know she needs help! Whether it's calling out to the Lord in prayer or calling a friend for encouragement, asking for help is a necessary part of parenting. Those can be humbling moments, requiring us to repent, then to confess to the Lord and our children our failure and sin. Or we might find ourselves rejoicing that we finally got it, praising God for the victory. When we ask for help or thank the Lord for His help, our daughters see our relationship with Jesus in action. And they will pick up and repeat our habits, behaviors, and words.

You are the one who models most of your baby's "firsts." You smile, and your baby returns your smile. You tell her to say "Momma," and pretty soon that is one of her first words. Later, you yell at the dog, and she repeats what you said perfectly! As she grows, she will watch you modeling faithfully the joy of praying for others.

Brandy learned this lesson very early when it came to perceiving her daughter Hannah's heart for prayer.

Brandy's Story: Discovering a Heart to Pray

The following excerpt comes from the journal Brandy has kept since Hannah Laynne was born. Brandy plans to give this journal to Hannah when she reaches the age of eighteen. When she wrote this entry on March 16, 2009, Hannah was two and a half years old.

My Sweetest Hannah,

Mommy had a headache for two days (I'm dealing with lots of discouragement!). However, tonight as we played together on the couch you asked, "Mommy, are you not feeling good?" Oh, you are so sweet! You immediately prayed and asked God to make my headache go away. I opened my eyes and you kissed my head and immediately my headache vanished! How precious, that God worked through you to touch and heal me of that terrible pain. I am so blessed!

By the time she turned three, Hannah became well known as the "finder" in Brandy's large family, and she's held that role ever since. Brandy says, "With all the demands of a household of seven, which includes my husband and my parents who live with us, I get quite distracted and invariably can't locate something when we start to leave the house. Whether it's keys, the baby's other shoe, the favorite cuddly blanket, or my phone, I immediately recruit the entire household, including my three daughters, who are seventeen, seven, and three. So often I'm at my wit's end when seven-year-old Hannah says, 'Let's pray, Mommy!'"

Hannah's faith humbles her mom, because Brandy knows praying is the first thing *she* should do. She says, "Hannah's childlike faith is exactly what I need, and I am blessed every time she turns to our heavenly Father and asks for His divine help. Amazingly, we always find whatever is lost. Always!"

Recently, Hannah's best friend, Serenity, lost a bag full of "special treasures" while the two families played at the park. All seven kids and two moms couldn't find the bag that was supposedly put into baby brother's stroller. They hoped it would show up somewhere.

The group piled into their vans and left for lunch. On the way Brandy shared with Serenity about the way God had answered Hannah's prayers so many times when things were lost. Did Serenity want Hannah to pray to find her bag of "special treasures?" Serenity said yes, so Hannah prayed. Before walking into the restaurant, everyone searched the cluttered vehicles again. But they came up empty.

During lunch, just as Serenity was about to pop a French fry into her mouth, she exclaimed, "I think I might have taken it to the big tree in the park!" The group raced back to the park. Lo and behold, right under the tree, they found Serenity's beloved bag of special treasures.

Brandy says, "We have watched Hannah's faithfulness grow, and we have seen the blessings of many answered prayers from our heavenly Father. Hannah's the first to pray, no matter how many times a day. She always smiles and begins each prayer with 'Thank you, God, for this wonderful day.'"

Hannah's faith is an inspiration both to her peers and to adults. I (Doreen) pray that this will continue throughout her lifetime.

How to Be a Perceiving Mom

Mothers like Brandy are blessed to perceive qualities and characteristics in their children from the very beginning. God's gift of perception especially helps new moms by letting them know, almost instinctively, when their babies are hungry, wet, or sleepy. This gift helps us meet our children's needs, protect them, and shape their growth.

To perceive means to observe, recognize, identify. Often it is easy to observe or recognize inherited family traits in our little ones. Sometimes unique features or characteristics of each child are clearly evident from birth. This results in familiar comments such as "She looks just like her daddy," or "She's twenty-two inches long. She's going to be a model just like her aunt Shelley." As a few months pass, other characteristics become evident. Maybe she is content to be alone for longer periods of time than her older brother could ever stand. Or she needs attention at every waking moment to be content. Fill in the blanks right now as you remember your own daughter in those early months or years of her life.

I am convinced that at an early age Hannah saw her momma pray. Brandy may have observed her own mother or grandmother pray and watched how they responded and expressed joy in answers to prayer. Therefore, Brandy recognized the value of modeling what she wanted her children to learn. It probably started with family prayers at dinner. Hannah might have imitated the way everyone bowed their heads and thanked God for the meal. Then as Hannah grew, her mom may have included her during her personal prayer time when she talked to her heavenly Father about people or concerns important to their family. Hannah may have heard and observed her momma's reaction when she excitedly shared prayer answers.

Can you see how God uniquely created Hannah's personality to perfectly embrace her passion to pray? In personality terms, Hannah is a Social Butterfly. Her story reveals that she loves people, loves to talk, and probably loves an audience. Her mother will want to work on her weaknesses, such as her tendency to exaggerate, desire to be the center of attention, or tendency to let tasks and projects go unfinished. Brandy, in her wisdom and prayerfulness, will guide Hannah to use her personality strengths to continue to bless others.

Princess of Faith

It's important to nurture a daughter's prayer life and Bible knowledge to help her be faithful to God. I (Karen) started devotions with my oldest daughter, Rebecca, before her first birthday. When she was three, I marveled at how she put her faith into action by sharing with her friends. The following is one example of how she used fun to share about Jesus.

Rebecca's Ornament–Making Fun

Rebecca rushed into the room with a few girls trailing behind. "Mom," she yelled, "my friends' dads are at sea too. They need to make ornaments too!"

I (Karen) nodded and pulled out more art supplies. We had begun decorating a small Christmas tree that would be full of ornaments by the time Dad returned from deployment. I hoped Jim would return before Christmas Day, but one search-and-rescue call had already delayed the ship.

Rebecca remained positive that Dad would return home by Christmas Day. With her strong Born Leader personality, she liked to take control. That evening we prayed for Dad's safe return in time to celebrate Christ's birth. Even though she was only three, Rebecca already understood that Jesus came at Christmas. She said, "Mom, Jesus is the newborn King. So I'm a princess."

"Yes, you are a daughter of the King."

"Then let's make crown ornaments tomorrow!"

We used toilet paper rolls and foil wrapping paper to make little crowns. Rebecca told all the girls they were princesses. They made colorful crown ornaments, and then we made paper crowns for them to wear. They paraded around the room following Rebecca.

After two months at sea, with an extra detour to rescue stranded boaters, Jim arrived home. Rebecca and her brother

Michael hugged him and followed him everywhere. Rebecca pointed out the Christmas tree, and he lifted her up to take a closer look at the ornaments. She chatted about each one she made and how it related to Jesus.

Jim pointed to a pinecone turkey and said, "I see a turkey with feathers. Why is that at the bottom of the tree?"

"Daddy, you missed Thanksgiving, and I wanted to show you the turkey I made."

"We can thank God every day. I'm thankful I'm with you now."

"Mommy was right. Every day can be Thanksgiving." She gave her dad a big hug.

Rebecca continued to grow as a child of God. She loved the idea of being a princess. We lived in Hawaii, so she dressed up in little gowns or muumuus and made flower leis and crowns. After Christmas we made a princess treasure box. She decorated a shoe box with foil gift wrap and glued a paper crown on the cover. She filled it with little reminders of what she read in the Bible. For example, she added a bird's feather she found after we read about how God cares for the sparrows and cares for her, too (see Matthew 10:29-32).

At age six, Rebecca rejoiced that she finally had a sister after two brothers. She taught her little sister about God, dressed her up, and helped her make a treasure box when Darlene was old enough. Darlene always bounced more and spoke louder than Rebecca. With her Social Butterfly personality, she loved taking out the treasures to dance and sing while holding them. She invited friends to dance to her favorite Christian songs.

Developing the Fruit of Faithfulness

To be faithful means to be full of faith or to be loyal. We want our daughters to embrace faith as part of daily life. We pray it will show in their actions. Rebecca showed her desire to share her faith by inviting friends to participate in faith-building devotional activities and sharing her spiritual treasure box. I felt joyful when I listened to her share her faith with her friends.

It's wonderful to help our daughters know the Lord at an early age. Do you recall a time in your childhood when you attended church, heard about Jesus, or shared in a Christmas tradition that inspired faith? If so, share those memories with your daughter. End each day by chatting about what happened and how you applied God's Word or showed a fruit of the Spirit in action.

Pray together. Pause to pray before leaving home to ask God's protection on your travel and day. Read a verse or Bible story together and talk about the meaning and application. Incorporate activities that use your daughter's strengths, such as Darlene's natural inclination to invite friends to dance and sing to her favorite Christian songs and the way Rebecca's treasure box made sharing her faith easy and natural.

Connecting a girl's prayer life with her personality makes prayer more natural. Rebecca, a natural Born Leader, liked to create her own prayers, pray at scheduled times, and share what she learned from devotions. Darlene preferred to sing praises for her prayer time. She was spontaneous and prayed anytime.

Use the tools that fit your daughter's abilities, interests, and personality.

Fruitful Activities

Following are some suggested activities that will help you guide your daughter to develop the attribute of prayer and the fruit of faithfulness.

Fruit of the Spirit Verse

"Let your roots grow down into him and draw up nourishment from him. See that you go on growing in the Lord, and become strong and vigorous in the truth you were taught. Let your lives overflow with joy and thanksgiving for all he has done" (Colossians 2:7, TLB).

Cultivating faith starts with planting seeds of truth about God in your daughter's heart and nurturing it with prayer.

Princess Treasure Box

Help your daughter make her own treasure box. Cover a shoe box and decorate it. Keep it in a special place. Add items as reminders of Bible stories, prayer answers, and God's love.

Examples:

- a feather as a reminder that God cares for birds (see Matthew 10:29-31)

- a bandage for Jesus healing someone

- a white pom-pom to represent a sheep, because Jesus is our Good Shepherd

- a heart sticker as a reminder of God's love

On the cover of the treasure box add the princess acrostic as a reminder of the virtues being developed as a daughter of the King:

- **P**rayerful
- **R**espectful
- **I**nspired
- **N**oble
- **C**ompassionate
- **E**ncourager
- **S**elf-controlled
- **S**ervant

Dishing Up Prayer

Fill a bowl with pictures or words related to God and things a girl can talk to God about. Each day let your daughter write a word (if she is older) or draw a picture (if she is younger), and discuss the topic. Then pray and ask God to take care of the person, creature, or object.

Prayer Journal

Give your grade-school-age daughter a prayer journal to record her prayers and answers to prayer. Encourage her to go back at times to read past prayer requests.

Princess Prayer ABCs

Work on these attributes with your daughter, one a day, or as desired.

- **A**ddress God with a greeting (say hello). Point out that the word *adore* means "to worship" and "to love." Let your daughter echo phrases such as "Dear Father, I love You" or "Creator, thanks for making me." "You can do anything! You are almighty."

- **B**elieve in Jesus and tell Him you believe in Him.

- **C**onfess sins. As a powerful illustration, start by getting your hands dirty together, then washing them. As the water cleans your hands, explain how that's a picture of the way God cleans our hearts. He washes our hearts when we confess our sins. Talk about how it's wrong to disobey rules.

- **D**elight in God. Tell Him you love Him. Be happy about all the things God does. Talk about animals and people God made. Thank Him for each one.

- **E**xpress your thoughts. Talk to God, and tell Him what you are thinking. Also tell Him about your problems, and ask for His help.

- **F**ind new ways each day to show love to one another as God has asked us to do.

- **G**ive thanks. Name blessings with your daughter, and thank God for each one. (Include things like family, home, clothes, toys, food.)

- **H**and over your hurts by letting God know your problems. When your daughter feels sad or hurt, pause and pray. Let her tell God how she feels.

- **I**nvite the Holy Spirit to guide you. Talk about how the Holy Spirit gives your daughter gifts and fruits like love, joy, and peace. Pray with her for God's Holy Spirit to guide both of you today in making wise choices.

- **J**ournal. Help your daughter start a simple journal where she can draw and write about God and her prayers. She can read through it and star answered prayers. She can also read it as a prompt to pray.

- **K**eep knocking (asking). Talk about prayers that you continue to pray every day and still want God to answer. Don't give up. Keep praying. Find a visual reminder, such as a doorknob. When you look at it, remember to pray again.

- **L**isten. Pause and sit quietly to listen to God. Open the Bible and read His words. They are love letters.

- **M**ean what you say. Encourage your daughter to be honest with God. Urge her to tell Him the truth when she does something wrong. Remind her that it's okay to share how she feels, even when she is sad or angry.

- **N**otice blessings. Each day, remember the good things that happened and all that God provided. Thank Him for each blessing. Help your daughter thank God for each sense and a related blessing, such as thanking Him for her sense of hearing and a new song.

- **O**ffer your talents to God. Point out that friends help one another. Explain that God is also your friend and wants you to help Him by loving other people. Talk with your daughter about her talents and how she can use them to help God. Pray for God to give her opportunities to use her talents.

- **P**raise the Lord. Admire God for who He is. Let your child echo your prayerful praises and clap after each one. Say things such as "God, You made the world. You are so great." Or "God, You answer prayers. You are so good and loving!"

- **Q**uiet down and listen. Pause and listen again for God to bring peace and joy into your heart. Listen for His answers.

- **R**ead and pray through the Bible. Read God's love letters. Try reading a psalm each day to your daughter, and let her echo some of the words as a prayer.

- **S**eek help for others. Pray for family and friends. Pray for people everywhere to know God. Pray for peace.

- **T**rust that God knows best. Believe God will answer your prayers. Ask Him to guide you. Wait for His timing. Waiting a long time means to persevere, so be ready to keep trusting and persevering. Pray for help to be patient while waiting. Tell God you trust Him.

- **U**nite your will to God's. Help your princess allow God to change her heart and mind. He can bring peace when we don't get our way and help us understand that His way is better. Pray with your daughter that God will change your hearts when needed.

- **V**alue God and value how He made you! With your daughter, talk to God about how important He is in your life. Choose as you pray to follow Him and His words. Be thankful for the way He made you. Remember that He does not make mistakes.

- **W**orship God. Explain that one of the Greek words for *worship* means "to kiss or lick"—like a dog licks its master's hand. Say great things about God, then blow Him kisses. Examples of things to say might include "Lord Jesus, You are my Shepherd and You guide me." Or "Lord, You are the King and my Rock."

- **X**-ray your heart by actively listening. As you end your prayer time, listen again. Explain that a conversation means to take turns talking. Listen for God's words. Also, let God "x-ray" your heart to be sure it's full of love. Ask God to show you any anger or hurt still there, and ask Him to heal your heart.

- **Y**earn to grow in grace. Pray with your daughter to ask God to help her keep growing in grace and to keep learning more about Him.

- **Z**ealously end with the desire to return. In other words, say, "We'll talk again." Tell God you will be happy to pray again. Be thankful for the time you spent praying.

Using Prayer ABCs

When you pray with your daughter, you can focus on a few of the ABC attributes of prayer. For each one, discuss what it means and practice implementing the idea. For example, **A** is for "Address God with a greeting." Practice ways to greet God (Dear Father, Almighty King, Our Father, Lord, Jesus, etc.).

Write each ABC of prayer on a separate card. Draw one out when you want to pray.

Make an ABC prayer book. Use the words for each letter to make a page. Add images to help your child recall the meaning. A telephone could be used for a greeting. A cross could be on the page for **B** and "Believe in Jesus."

Dad and Daughter Activities

Daily Dad Prayer Time

Dads, once you get home (or via the Internet or phone if you're traveling), chat with your daughter. Ask about her day and what she did. Ask about any problems. Hold her hands and pray with her. If you'll be away and out of touch, give her a journal to draw or write in about her day. Look through it together when you return.

Your Presence While Away

For dads who travel or who are on deployments, stay connected. Record yourself reading a book or telling a story. Your wife can turn the recording on once your child is settled and ready for bed.

If you are home every day, you might still want to record a few books for your daughter to hear your voice or have quiet time listening to you.

Mom's Tools

Faithfulness and Personality

Foster your daughter's faith according to her personality. It will be more natural for her depending on her unique needs and preferences. The following ideas show how you can personalize faith-building activities based on your princess's personality type.

A *Social Butterfly* likes making friends.

- Talk about a personal friendship with Jesus.

- Read the book of Esther to discover how the king needed a new queen, so he held a beauty pageant. Discuss Esther's beauty pageant and the way she gave parties.

- Be spontaneous with prayer, and let your daughter make up her own prayers.

A *Born Leader* wants a plan.

- Read about strong biblical leaders such as Deborah, who served as a judge in Old Testament times. Talk about David, the king of Israel, and the apostle Paul.

- Read about Martha, the sister of Mary and Lazarus, who stayed busy and sometimes forgot to sit and listen when Jesus visited (see Luke 10:38-42).

- Make prayer part of your daily routines (before meals, leaving home, at bedtime).

A *Princess of Order* likes a sense of direction and prefers to be a disciple (follower).

- Talk about a personal friendship with Jesus and what it means to follow Him.

- Share how we as people are like sheep and Jesus is the Good Shepherd described in Psalm 23.

- Read about quiet followers such as Esther and Mary, the mother of Jesus.

- Pray simple Scriptures that she can repeat after you.

Everyone's Friend likes humor, peace, and being beloved.

- Share about God's love and forgiveness by reading Matthew 6:14-15. Talk about being forgiven by God if you forgive others. Read Ephesians 4:32 and discuss being tenderhearted to forgive. Practice saying the Lord's Prayer.

- Read from the Gospel of John, which talks about God's love.

- Read stories that show compassion or peacemaking, such as the parable of the Good Samaritan who cared for a stranger he found hurt on the roadside (see Luke 10:30-37).

Mom's Journaling Observations

Observing your daughter is key to understanding her. Purchase a diary or create an online journal file. Start recording your observations about the characteristics you notice in your daughter.

Assess your daughter's personality and record it. Notice when she acts out of her personality style, and write down what you can do to bring out the best in her.

Observe and answer these types of questions:

- What makes her smile?

- What makes her sad?

- How does she relate to other people?

- When is she comfortable talking?

- How does she solve problems?

Ask her questions to discover more about her passions and interests:

- Would you like to play outside with a ball or take a walk?

- Would you like to cook something or make something?

- What's your favorite book?

Dad's Toolbox

The first tool my dad placed in his toolbox as he prepared for a project was his favorite hammer, made of forged steel. It was heat treated for maximum strength; its handle was slip resistant, and it came with a lifetime warranty.

Think of how that special tool equates to the prayers that you will hammer into heaven, with maximum strength, to be nailed into your daughter's life as you pray for her. Consider your own life—and hers. We know that our lives will also be heat treated, encountering stress and pressure. As you persevere, you will discover your maximum strength as you grow in Christ and continue to share the strength of your faith with her. Yes, potential slips will come. Conversely, you will be slip resistant as you continue over the years to pray for her, guaranteeing a well-built, Christ-centered life.

Each generation has been an education for us in different ways. The first child-with-bloody-nose was rushed to the emergency room. The fifth child-with-bloody-nose was told to go to the yard immediately and stop bleeding on the carpet.

ART LINKLETTER, author of *Kids Say the Darndest Things*

3

The Fruit of Peace
in Your Princess's Life

*La Belle Jardinière must refine the soil by removing
rocks and debris, then tilling it to loosen it and
make the dirt soft and pliable for seeds to grow.*

Refining Mothers
Princess Attribute—Respect
Fruit of the Spirit—Peace

THINK ABOUT THE TASK OF polishing a beautiful silver pitcher
that has become badly tarnished. First, you have to locate a
bottle of silver polish. Then you rummage through a bag
of rags to find the softest cloth for the job. You grab the
old dishtowel cloth, knowing it's what you need to get the
job done well. Then you go to work polishing the pitcher.
Soon it is shining beautifully, free of tarnish and refined to
its original beauty.

In some ways, being a mother is like polishing silver.
A mother uses the right tools and applies her loving elbow
grease to polish (or refine) her daughter. A daughter will learn
to respect the discipline that is sometimes necessary to rub
out the tarnished areas of her behavior. Her refined character

37

will bring peace of mind to her mother, father, and others in her life. And this budding princess will experience peace in her own heart as she begins to respect others.

Brandy's Story: Breaking Behavior

As moms, we all have our weak moments. Doreen's daughter Brandy shares a story that has roots in her own childhood.

Some of my funniest memories include times my family spent together in the car. When I was little, my dad employed linguistic inventiveness to keep from using bad words about other drivers when their poor driving habits were evident on the road. Some of my favorites were "yo-yo," "ding-dong," "slick," and "yardbird." These names sounded silly and made us laugh as my dad channeled his irritation through mild name-calling. But it had a long-range impact.

Recently, I drove my three children to homeschool academy, rushing once again. Suddenly, I slammed on my brakes and immediately felt frustrated at quite a large woman in a rather small car going too slowly. I commented (with the windows fully rolled up), "Come on and put some of that weight on the pedal." That immediately prompted my oldest daughter to giggle as we sped past the woman's car.

Later in the day I felt discouraged as I struggled with my daughter's disrespectful attitude. I observed her sense of superiority and disrespect toward her sister. In my moment of frustration about her behavior, wondering what to do next, the Holy Spirit called me up short. I immediately realized that my daughter's words reflected the same attitude I displayed earlier that very day. I sadly realized that when I am driving the car, too often I display disrespect too.

A display about our family's identity hangs on our family's dining room wall. About ten years ago we created an acronym using Corea, our last name. In my reflective moment, I happened to glance at this display as I was pondering my downfall.

Confident . . . in God
Obedient . . . to God and others
Respectful . . . to God, others, and myself
Excellence . . . strive for excellence in all things
Adaptability . . . in all situations

As you can see, the letter "R" stands for "Respectful to God, others, and myself." I realized immediately how badly I was missing the mark I had helped set for our children. I felt convicted that respect was something I needed to work on. The Lord gently reminded me that I am called to model the fruit of the Spirit before my children, and that I am normally their first view of what respect should look like!

Then I glanced at our chalkboard where we post verses we are memorizing. There it was: "Do not let any unwholesome talk come out of your mouths, but only what is helpful for building others up according to their needs, that it may benefit those who listen" (Ephesians 4:29, NIV).

Though seemingly lighthearted, my comments in the car didn't show the respect that everyone deserves. God's Word reminds us to respect others, and I am calling my own children to do that too. That conviction brought me to my knees. Today I'm trying my best to be sure that humor is not at the expense of someone else. More often now I just laugh at myself; there's plenty of material there to fill a book!

How to Be a Refining Mom

To be refining moms, we must recognize our own personal need to remove the impurities within our hearts. We must admit our own faults, our sins, and ask God's forgiveness. When necessary, we must apologize to people we hurt and repair relationships.

To refine our daughters, we need to discipline them, teach them ladylike behavior, and help them learn to apologize and to forgive others.

The definition of *refine* is "to cultivate, enhance, purify—to make free from impurities."

I (Doreen) believe that one of the greatest honors God gives us is the opportunity to become a mother. Certainly God Himself holds this role in His highest esteem. He recognized a mother's value and position in the Ten Commandments.

"Honor your father and your mother, that your days may be long in the land that the LORD your God is giving you" (Exodus 20:12, ESV). Did you know that this is the only one of the Ten Commandments with a promise? Yet it also comes with the highest calling we will have in our lives.

Stop with me for just a moment and reminisce about some of those precious moments involving your first child's birth. Remember savoring those moments when your baby finally fell asleep in your arms? Think about how much you enjoyed the sweet smell of your nursing infant, the warmth of his or her touch on your face for the first time. Or when your little one recognized you as Mommy, wanting only you. Recall the fun and excitement of those first steps and first words. Did you, as I did, cherish every one of those moments as a gift?

As I consider God's words about our children—such as "Children are a gift from God" (Psalm 127:3, TLB)—I am reminded of other gifts I have valued highly over the years. (Maybe you've felt this way too.) Could it be that your heart, too, was deeply warmed and tears filled your eyes as you received a special gift from your grandmother? Maybe you placed it in a box of memorable treasures, a safe place. Could it be a lovely piece of jewelry that will need to be gently handled and cleaned after it has been proudly worn? Or did you ever receive a beautifully flowering plant that needed to be fed, watered, and cultivated to continue growing and blooming? Think about how it gave you great pleasure each time you saw it and remembered the giver.

No matter what kind of gift you or I have been given, if it is of value to us, we will care for it. Because children are a gift from God, He holds us accountable for caring for them as the special treasures they are. Brandy's story certainly illustrates that. The Lord spoke to Brandy's heart because of the way her negative behavior was already influencing her daughter's behavior.

Can you see how the Lord desires that we be refiners for our little girls? Some women are by nature more nurturing. Others learn the value of nurturing over time and begin to appreciate the fruit that it bears when we are willing to be refined by the hand of God. He will equip us to raise the children we birthed, adopted, or fostered. There may be moments in every mom's life when she would beg to differ (including me), but He will help us do our best.

To be a refiner, first recognize your need to be refined and be willing to go through the process. Our hearts need to be refined first so that we can then become refiners.

I shopped at Macy's for the first time when I was about eighteen. I was so excited to be in a high-end store all by myself. I found a blouse I actually could afford and went to the cashier's counter to wait in line. I noticed a woman at the head of the line, one of the most refined women I had ever seen. With perfect hair and makeup, she wore a lovely cashmere sweater and matching skirt. She carried a name-brand purse and sported lovely high-heeled shoes. I was wowed—wishing someday I might look and dress just like that woman. But after several minutes the cashier finally arrived and the woman immediately started to yell, unleashing foul language on the poor cashier. She pounded her hand on the counter, then left in a huff.

It was the first time in my life I'd ever seen the beauty

of a woman fall before my very eyes. Her face appeared to change into that of a wicked witch's, and I backed away when she stomped by me. She actually scared me, yet she never even looked my way. The way she dressed made a good first impression. However, what came out of her mouth destroyed any perceived grace or beauty I'd thought she had.

I came home that day anxious to tell my mother the story. Her sweet and gentle spirit refreshed me as she listened patiently to every detail. When I finished, she said with a heart of compassion, "Who knows what she has been through?"

I didn't yet have the spiritual maturity to look beyond that woman's appearance and see her pain, suffering, or possible rejection that caused rocks in the soil of her heart. Only God knew what must have wounded her, and that day my mom demonstrated a heart of a refiner.

The only way we will remove the sticks and stones of unforgiveness or poor behavior in our own lives and our daughters' lives is to keep the soil of our hearts watered with the Word of God. In addition, stay accountable to others. Ask them to mention any weeds of ungodly words or behaviors that they observe, so that you can continue to grow in the fruit of the Spirit. Establish a pattern of holding your daughter accountable and reading the Bible together.

As you are called to live in a manner that leads your daughter to become a beautiful princess—a daughter of the King—try to take a few minutes each day to hear someone speak God's Word online, listen to a worship song or two, or sing a simple song of praise to your little princess. His Word is the best refining process we have that will enable peace to resonate in your heart and home.

You, the refiner, can be used by God to remove stubborn rocks, in the form of sinful behaviors that are like weeds in the heart of a princess. But as you till the soil of her heart with your words and actions, the Holy Spirit will cause the seeds to grow and bear fruit.

Princess of Peace

A child's cry or whine quickly disrupts the peace. Peace is not a natural character trait of a little girl who wants to get her way. It didn't take long for me (Karen) to discover my eldest daughter's strong-willed spirit. The importance of cultivating peace was very clear when it came to my first daughter, Rebecca.

Rebecca's Tantrum

The weather turned cooler and the leaves changed colors, so I took my two-year-old daughter shopping for a warm coat. We found a blue one with fur trim. She tried it on and smiled in front of the mirror. But when it was time to pay and I took it off her, she screamed.

I said, "Honey, we have to pay for the coat. Do you want to carry it?"

She continued screaming. I waited for her to stop. Shoppers stared. My daughter fell on the floor, screaming louder. I said, "Rebecca, calm down. I love you."

I was expecting a baby and unable to just remove her from the store. She finally stopped screaming and simply sobbed. I asked her to get up and she did. She grabbed for the coat, but I gently rehung it.

I whispered, "You're too upset and tired to buy anything today. We'll go home to rest. We'll come back on a happier day." I held her hand and thanked the clerk for her patience.

In the car Rebecca stuttered between sobs, "I w-wanted that b-blue c-coat."

I replied, "You were not a young lady with all that screaming. But tomorrow is a brand-new day for you to be a little princess and buy a coat."

The next day, Rebecca said she was sorry she screamed in the store. We talked about how she had felt angry and sad. I thanked her and asked her to tell God she was sorry. I explained that we would return and see if they still had that coat, but she would need to apologize to the clerk.

My daughter asked, "What if they sold the coat?"

I said, "That would mean God had other plans for that coat. We will thank God that another girl would be warm and like the coat. Then, we'll find one God wants for you." She nodded. We talked about how her tantrum did not show respect to the shoppers, the clerk, God, or me. She asked if we could shop at a different store, but I said we had to apologize. I agreed that people had stared, but it didn't give her what she wanted.

We got in the car and prayed. We drove to the store, and Rebecca said she was sorry to the workers she saw. They graciously accepted her apology. Then she danced to the coat section and spotted the blue coat. She said, "Mommy, it's still here!"

We bought it, and she thanked the clerk. Our second outing turned out to be more peaceful than the previous one! Rebecca never had a tantrum in a store again. Each time before we shopped, I asked, "Are you ready to be an agreeable and peaceful lady?" We started to pray in the car before leaving home, and that made a big difference.

Developing the Fruit of Peace

As a mother of five, I (Karen) have experienced many moments of chaos, tantrums, and squabbles. It didn't take long to discover that real peace only comes from hearts filled with love that learn to forgive and eliminate anger, jealousy, and other negative emotions.

Peace denotes calmness, freedom from quarrels, and the absence of war or violence. Sometimes your beautiful daughter may go into a rage for unknown reasons. It might be exhaustion, allergies, sickness, or feeling overwhelmed. Giving in reinforces negative behavior. It's easy to feel embarrassed and yell, but that's not peaceful. Remaining calm, using a gentle voice, and waiting for the child to regain control of her emotions helps. Remove your child to a quiet place, if possible. Let the incident become a teachable moment after your daughter calms down. Observe what may trigger tantrums to help your child avoid them. I recall feeling helpless at the first tantrum, but soon discovered that helping my daughter regain her composure worked best.

Peace flows from a heart that is full and satisfied. Someone who feels unwanted or unnoticed clamors for attention with whining, jealous reactions, and arguing. Be sure to take time to express and show love. Praise your daughter's efforts and not simply results. Let her know she is important to God. Let her know you embrace her as God made her and that you want the best for her. Yes, it's important to grow those fruits, but her worth isn't measured through grades or winning games.

It's hard to apologize, but forgiveness brings peace. Be willing to say you are sorry when you hurt your child's feelings to show that you value forgiveness. Help your daughter notice how someone else reacted to her words or actions. For example, say something like "Look at how Pam is crying and rubbing her shoulder where you punched her. A punch can really hurt. I know she is your friend and you care about her. It's not good to punch. It's time to say you are sorry and that you hope she feels better." That builds respect for the other person and helps children learn to reconcile and build stronger friendships.

Sit quietly with your daughter to listen to nature and enjoy a peaceful day or the beauty of silence. That fosters respect for God's creation and helps girls understand tranquility. End your days by thanking God for His help with respecting others. As your daughter makes an effort to control her emotions and honor other people, she will become a peacemaker.

Fruitful Activities

Fruit of the Spirit Verse

"So let us do all we can to live in peace. And let us work hard to build each other up" (Romans 14:19).

Respect promotes the fruit of peace. Working for peace includes not saying unkind words and apologizing for hurtful actions and words. Fill your girl's heart with love. Root out anger with forgiveness, and help her learn to share and care for others.

R-E-S-P-E-C-T

Post this acrostic as a reminder of respectful behavior. Help your daughter find and add pictures (such as an ear for *listening*), especially if she does not yet read.

R-eally listen.
E-xpress respect with words (please, thank you, excuse me).
S-peak in a gentle or enthusiastic and positive tone.
P-raise the other person.
E-njoy the uniqueness of the person (differences, interests, abilities).
C-hoose to use good manners.
T-hink before you speak or act.

Family Identity Wall Hanging

Create your family identity wall hanging. Using each letter of your last name, list an adjective or a word that begins with that letter in a sentence that expresses the godly traits you've observed in your family. Include traits from your grandparents, parents, spouse, spouse's heritage, yourself, or even your children. Then consider Christlike characteristics you desire to see in the heart of your family. Pray together and choose one element from the list for each letter.

This is a wonderful step toward establishing a family legacy. You can refer to Brandy's story for an example, or check out this example:

S-erving others first.
M-aking our home an honorable and fun place to live.
I-nvesting in things that will make a difference.
T-aking God's Word into our hearts daily.
H-eeding correction that reveals a teachable spirit.

Once you prayerfully decide on words that describe your family identity, create your wall hanging. Here are three suggested methods:

1. The simplest approach is to create it on a computer using a favorite large font, print it out, and slide the printout into a frame.

2. Print the acrostic from your computer on 8½-by-11-inch paper. Laminate it. Cut a piece of wood 9½ by 12 inches or locate one that size. Stain or paint the wood to match the decor of the room where you plan to hang it. Center the paper on the wood and glue it in place.

3. Sew a quilt patch with your family identity stitched on it. You can print the identity on fabric to use in the quilt, use fabric markers, or embroider it. Add hanging loops and purchase a dowel to hang it on.

Display the family identity in a location where family members will see it daily.

Treasure Box Addition

Remember the treasure box from the last chapter? Add an item to help your daughter remember the importance of respect.

Read about two women who respected God in Exodus 1:15-21. Talk about how the women saved the Israelite babies when Pharaoh didn't want them to have more sons. God blessed them with their own children. Place a tiny baby doll inside the treasure box to remind your daughter to respect God and people.

Happy Hearts

When your daughter gets angry or refuses to apologize, let her cool down. Then discuss happy hearts: Does she want a happy heart? Does she want other people to have happy hearts? Talk about how apologizing, sharing, and making others happy puts sparkle and smiles in her heart.

Respect for the Bible (Make a Crown Bookmark)

To show respect for God and His Word, help your daughter find a special place to keep her Bible.

Help your little princess make a crown bookmark as a reminder to respect the Bible.

- Cut the corner from an envelope to form a triangle with 2½-inch sides.

- Cut out small triangles from the sides to form a crown.

- On one side write "God the King."

- On the other side write "Princess (name)."

- Open the triangle and slide it over the corner of a page.

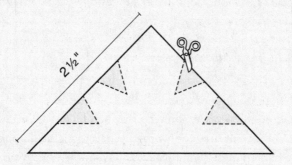

Fruit of Peace Bingo

I counted my ten fingers when I felt angry.	I shared my toys.	I took turns.	I remembered to say please and thank you.	I prayed for my friends.
I calmed down and then talked about a problem.	I waited for my turn.	! let Mommy talk on the phone and played quietly.	I thanked a friend for playing with me.	I let a friend have the first turn.
When I did not agree I talked about it without yelling.	I listened with my eyes.	I listened with my ears.	My heart is happy.	I felt angry but closed my eyes and thought a happy thought.
I forgave someone who hurt my feelings.	I opened the door for someone.	When I felt angry I stopped and prayed.	When someone called me a name I remained silent (that's not my name).	I was angry but still used good words.
I know I am loved.	I know God loves me.	I told the truth when I did something wrong.	I picked up litter to respect the world God made.	I was kind to someone.

Dad and Daughter Activities

Dad and Tea Parties

A tea party is a great opportunity for your daughter to discover how a gentleman should treat a lady. Be sure to:

- Escort her to the room.

- Pull out a chair for her.

- Compliment her.
- Listen and carry on a conversation.

Meals with Daughters

Let every meal become an opportunity to set an example by complimenting the cook, conversing, and using good manners.

Woodworking

Make a woodworking project with your daughter. Sign up for a workshop at a local hardware store if you don't have tools. As you sand the wood, talk about the gentle but firm touch that makes the wood smooth. Talk about how correcting her makes her a better person, smoothing away the roughness of anger, selfishness, and other bumpy behavior.

Mom's Tools

Fostering Self-Respect

It's important for a child to have self-respect and to know she is precious.

- Remind her that she is a child of God, who loves her.
- Tell her she is kind, creative, smart, and so on when she displays those character traits.
- Give her time to look her best and to care for her clothes by helping with laundry.
- Praise her good grooming habits.
- Help her choose foods that promote health.
- Exercise with her to care for her body.

- Remind her that she does not have to believe teasing, but can state the truth (i.e., I am smart but sometimes I make mistakes).

- Give sincere compliments to your daughter.

Modeling Respect

- Before making phone calls spend time with your child. Meet her needs and let her know you have a call to make.

- Speak about loved ones with respect and avoid gossip.

- If your child complains about your spouse or another adult, remind her that you love and respect that person, then list his or her good qualities.

- Be polite. Always thank your daughter for giving you something, obeying you, or spending time with you.

- When your child has a problem, listen. Ask what she thinks would solve it. This helps your daughter to find solutions and to know that you are listening.

- Before asking a child to do something, check what she is doing. Gently ask her to do the task when she stops or in five minutes.

- Ask why when your child repeats a poor behavior. If she colors on the wall, does she need more paper or an easel? If she's breaking eggs on the floor, does she want to learn to cook?

Bless Your Child

Blessing your child shows you value her. Hold a blessing party. Place your hand on her head and pray for God's blessing. Write her a letter that praises her for who she is and her positive character traits.

Refining Steps

1. Establish a rule and discuss its importance (i.e., no TV or electronics during homework time helps each person to focus on the work).

2. Reward your daughter when she follows the rules (use a sticker or simply words of praise) and set a logical consequence for breaking a rule (such as no TV or electronics for an additional hour if she turned something on during homework time).

3. Refine according to her personality to bring out strengths and overcome weaknesses.

4. Observe your daughter in various situations, then talk together about what "grade" she would give herself for self-discipline, respecting others, and respecting authority. Discuss how well she observes rules at school, at home, and in groups. Talk about courtesy, orderliness, and conduct also. If any fall below "satisfactory," encourage her to work on them with your help.

Personality and Promoting Respect

Refine your daughter according to her personality using the following ideas based on specific needs.

A *Social Butterfly's* need for attention can distract her from being respectful.

- Time-outs remove her from vying for attention and socializing.

- Social interaction (having a friend over to play) is a good motivator.

- She needs to follow through and focus on simple goals.

- She likes you to watch her do tasks, and younger ones enjoy stickers as rewards.

A *Born Leader* can forget God wants us to respect others.

- Losing control can be her biggest fear.

- Giving her new responsibility is a great reward and motivator.

- Avoid arguing and focus on her goals and routines.

- Remind her to be considerate.

A *Princess of Order* has a tendency to be respectful, but she can be whiny sometimes.

- Patiently answer her questions and "whys."

- Help her accept something less than perfection.

- Encourage her to speak up and share ideas.

- She likes leaders who show her how to do tasks.

Everyone's Friend will respect others to keep the peace.

- She may need the reward of peace and relaxation to overcome procrastination.

- Jokes and humor motivate her.

- She will follow rules to keep the peace.

- Break projects and work into small tasks to overcome procrastination.

Dad's Toolbox

Chad's collection always included power tools. One key tool for success was a power sander. When I happened to be in his shop one day, I watched him prepare to sand down a knot on a piece of lumber. As I cautiously watched him approach the knot, I feared the sander might slip out of his grasp. But his strong hand guided the sander right over the bump several times, and soon the knot was smoothed to the level of the surrounding wood. Peace replaced my fear as I saw Chad's ability to guide and use the tool wisely.

Just like the sander, your respect for the power God has granted you for your family will be key to removing some of the knots in your daughter's life. Little girls sometimes will show a lack of respect. As you model respect toward her mom, she will learn to follow your example. Remember, it may require several tries to smooth out a knot. When the feel of the knot is gone, it will bring a great sense of peace.

As your daughter learns to respect "power-sander tool" moments, she will also discover the wonderful alternative: peace.

It's better for girls to be single but not for boys.
Boys need someone to clean up after them.

ANITA, age 9, quoted on Pinterest

The Fruit of Joy in Your Princess's Life

Once seeds are planted, La Belle Jardinière
continually waters the seeds and lets sunshine
inspire the growth.

Inspiring Mothers
Princess Attribute—Inspired
Fruit of the Spirit—Joy

JOY IS A DEEP SENSE OF continuing pleasure in God and trusting Him. People filled with joy have hearts overflowing with a positive attitude in spite of their circumstances. They sprinkle gladness into the lives of others. Joy helps us look forward to the future with a sense of hope.

We cannot simply give joy to a daughter, but we can inspire joy as we open her mind to dreaming about the future God has planned. We can inspire our princess to fearlessly try new things and tap in to her creative imagination. We can inspire our girl to think beyond what she can see and touch in order to grasp the joy she will someday experience in heaven. The following story comes from Karen's childhood, when one of her grandmothers inspired her.

Karen's Story: A Box of Imagination

On a snowy February day, ignoring the large, delicate snow-flakes falling to the ground, I (Karen) trudged through knee-deep snow to Grandma's house, seeking relief from boredom. I arrived at Grandma's, then removed my soggy clothes and dried off in front of a glowing fire. I sipped hot tea with her and savored the last few chocolates from the Valentine's Day box. Then I peered into the box and lamented, "It's empty."

Grandma looked inside the container and declared, "Why, you must have lost your eyesight. This box looks quite full."

I blinked and searched again but found no candy. Grandma giggled and carefully removed some of the contents.

She was right. The box was far from empty. The carton held little brown papers that we soon transformed into lamp-shades, table skirts, doll bonnets, collars, and skirts. From her craft drawer, or "imagination cupboard," as Grandma called it, she produced large buttons for heads and pipe cleaners to twist into dolls that modeled the latest fashion creations.

We snipped the cardboard that once separated layers of chocolates into frames for tiny pictures we cut from old magazines. From larger pieces of cardboard we cut tabletops and attached wooden spool legs.

Last, and most wonderful of all, we transformed the box itself into a treasure chest. It took hours, padding the box with quilt batting and covering it with ice-pink satin fabric scraps. We added lace trim, glued on beads and sequins, then lined the inside with black velvet.

I stayed overnight because one day wasn't long enough to finish the projects Grandma and I dreamed up. As though seeing snowflakes for the first time, I saw the beauty in each exquisite creation. Through the eyes of Grandma, I encountered a new world, one limited only by my imagination.

When I had my own children, I gave them each an imagination box filled with ribbons, fabric scraps, art supplies, clay, and other supplies. They pulled them out anytime they wanted to make something. My older daughter loved making her own books and projects for her imaginary students.

One day Darlene, my younger daughter, lamented, "My imagination is much bigger than my box." She often asked me to buy her more glitter, paper, markers, and glue. She snipped off scraps of ribbon and fabric from my remnants. She loved collecting items for her imagination box, and it tended to overflow.

We purchased a large wooden cabinet as a new imagination place and quickly filled it with more scraps and supplies. My daughter's friends enjoyed raiding it for school projects and creative fun. Now Darlene has her own daughters and an imagination room—as her cabinet spilled over and needed more space. Her daughters love gathering supplies and transforming objects into treasured artwork. It seems a child simply opens the door and becomes inspired as his or her imagination begins to whirl.

How to Be an Inspiring Mom

Mothering beckons us to bring out the best in our daughters and to help them fearlessly follow the plans God has for them. We want to promote a sense of adventure. We also want to help them be hopeful, so joy will grow in their hearts.

To *inspire* means "to fill with courage and strength of purpose; to stimulate energies and ideas."

God is the source of inspiration. When we say the Bible is inspired, we mean it is God-breathed. He has plans for a child before her birth and weaves those into her very being. It is an honor as a parent to encourage or inspire our daughters. We have the opportunity to open their minds and hearts to fearlessly use their imaginations and overcome obstacles to persevere in spite of challenges.

Reflect on times your child came running to show you something she made or to sing words she strung together to create her own song. Have you watched your daughter play and seen how she brings her dolls and toys to life in her mind? Have you applauded her determination to master a skill, from walking to riding a bicycle? Have you rejoiced in her success and marveled at her creativity?

Inspiring a girl goes beyond art, as we encourage our daughters to believe in the future and follow their dreams. This encouragement is an outgrowth of God's plan for each child: "I pray that out of his glorious riches he may strengthen you with power through his Spirit in your inner being" (Ephesians 3:16, NIV).

It is the inner being—the soul and spirit—that we want God to strengthen in our daughters. We want them to believe in God and His ability to work through them to do immeasurably more than all they can ask or imagine (see Ephesians 3:20).

Stifling a daughter's creativity begins with words that dismiss imaginative creations or toss out the wonders she's made. Thankfully, rejoicing over a new song, a picture, or game fosters her creative juices. Remember, it takes courage to overcome failures when we try something new and it doesn't work out as we envisioned.

There will be failures along the way, as well as people who use discouraging words or laugh at your child's creations. Thomas Edison once responded to a remark that he had failed by saying, "I have gotten a lot of results. I know several thousand things that won't work."

Edison persisted until he found what worked. Failure is simply an experiment in learning. Stories of people who overcame difficulties inspire us, especially those stories that spring from our own family trees. Hearing these stories will boost your daughter's confidence.

Marie faced discouraging words, for instance, when her high school teacher said she'd have to switch classes and give up her regular college-bound studies and think about a trade. She had dreamed of being a nurse for years. She even walked to a library as a young teen to take a Red Cross class intended for adults. She pleaded that she wanted to be a nurse, so the teacher allowed her to stay and take the class. Her parents had prayed for her future. When they saw her tears and thought of the way she bandaged dolls and younger siblings, they chose to support and encourage her dream. They argued her case with the principal.

When told she might fail a grade, they responded, "So what if it takes her an extra year to graduate. Who are you to take away her dreams?" The principal gave in. Indeed, it did take Marie an extra year to graduate, but she became a registered nurse who loved her geriatric patients, and her patients loved her.

We influence our daughters through our words and reactions. Do you listen when your little girl explains her thoughts? Do you encourage her individuality?

Pause and think about the last time your daughter pulled up weeds to give you a dandelion bouquet, invited you to her imaginary tea party, made her own (sloppy but yummy) sandwich, wrote a story or play, or piled up blankets to make a castle. Did you snap a few photos, laugh, and join her fun? Or did you ignore her, busy with housework or texting a friend? When you rejoice with her, you foster her inner strength to pursue big dreams and give her reason to be filled with joy at following smaller dreams in the meantime.

You hold the power of words that will encourage or discourage your daughter. What will you choose? Will you continually lift your daughter up in prayer and ask God to strengthen her inner being with dreams that He will help her fulfill? Will you seek opportunities that help her develop skills to fulfill her dreams? Will your words show you believe in her? Will you inspire her to rejoice in God's creation to develop joy in her heart? I pray that you will remind her that God's power is unlimited, so she can dream big and be inspired with joy.

Princess of Joy

Moms are called to help discover and inspire good character as well as gifts and talents in our daughters' lives. Sometimes it requires discipline to cultivate good behavior that will lead to joy later. Oh, the joy in the heart of a mom when her daughter obeys upon the first request! A mom feels pleased when she motivates her daughter to discover and develop her gifts and talents. When her abilities are given or displayed, both hearts fill with joy.

Thanks for the Discipline!

I (Doreen) remember my oldest daughter, Brandy, at the age of two lying to me for the first time. I was in shock when I asked her why she had taken a little unbreakable vase I had placed on a lower shelf for the sole purpose of teaching obedience, having already instructed her not to touch it. Her answer was, "I didn't touch it!" She was right. She had done more than touch it. She had taken it to her room and hidden it! I don't know how she learned to lie. In that moment I recognized the sin nature of mankind, but I had never seen it so blatantly displayed in my child! Oh, the shock of being a new mom and realizing the responsibility that came in training my little ones in the way they should go.

My discipline that day was not pleasurable, nor did it bring happiness. However, it was a first step toward developing the fruit of joy as we prayed together and asked Jesus to forgive her.

The years flew by. One day, I remember my daughter Brandy coming home from high school and informing me that her English class was required to write an essay about moms. She said, "Mom, I want to thank you for every swat you ever gave me. I know you did it for my good, and I am a better and more joyful person today because of it." I stood there speechless and full of joy, knowing only God could have done that work in her heart. Why? Because I thought over the years I had at times given too harsh a swat or, on the other hand, was too tired to give one at all. But almost every day I focused on faithfully praying for her.

That day, the Lord gave me the privilege of experiencing unspeakable joy. Only He can change a heart. And we, as moms, have the privilege of watering the seeds of faith in our daughters' hearts and waiting to see the fruit of His Spirit appear in their lives.

Developing the Fruit of Joy

To inspire the fruit of joy in the heart of our little princesses, we must first reflect or rediscover it in our own lives. Most people are prone to think that *pleasure*, *happiness*, and *joy* are interchangeable. However, when we look in any dictionary, we quickly discover defining differences.

Pleasure is experienced from our physical senses—sight, sound, smell, taste, and touch.

Examples include:

- I love to swim. I'm going to go to the pool just to be refreshed.
- I enjoy the aroma of coffee brewing. I'm going to have a cup right now.
- I can hardly wait! I'm going for a massage today.

Happiness can be experienced through living out our character and values. Most of us feel happy when we have done the right thing.

- It felt good to be honest when I returned a wallet with more than $500 to the person who lost it.
- It just felt right to step up and publicly support the closing of our local abortion clinic.

Joy is ours as believers when we know our heavenly Father through His Son, Jesus Christ. Experiencing the blessings and positive changes in our lives, and our children's lives, comes with this wonderful relationship. Here are some examples:

- The first time you were able to care about someone who clearly disliked you.
- When you discovered a specific verse while reading your Bible that spoke directly to your situation and gave you the hope you needed that day.
- A speechless yet heartwarming moment when you saw a loved one for whom you had prayed, such as your daughter, accept Jesus Christ as her Savior.

You might be thinking, "How am I going to get my daughter to find real joy and not mere pleasure?" It is a process to develop joy in our children, even after they have accepted Jesus into their hearts. Joy comes with time and is a spiritual work that God accomplishes within their minds and hearts as they come to know Him. Be expectant. He is at work in your daughter's life, and *you* will experience some wonderful "joy sighting" moments as you watch her grow in her walk with Christ.

Fruitful Activities

The following activities will inspire your little girl's imagination and creativity. A mind and heart free to dream are more receptive to developing the fruit of joy.

Fruit of the Spirit Verse

"So don't be sad. The joy of the LORD makes you strong" (Nehemiah 8:10).

The joy described in this verse comes from a relationship with God. In Nehemiah's time, God's people cried because they realized they had sinned and failed to follow His Word. Nehemiah told them to stop weeping and reminded them that the joy of the Lord was their strength. He told them to celebrate, for they had chosen to listen to God's Word and that made the day holy. Joy came from God and from spending time in His Word.

When your daughter feels sad, read this verse or a psalm. Talk about how we can trust God and still have the joy of knowing He loves us even when we feel sad about a problem.

Princess Treasure Box Addition

Talk about Nehemiah 8:10, the fruit of the Spirit verse for this chapter, and the way joy comes from God. Consider adding a sparkling item to the treasure box as a reminder of real joy.

Joy Sparklers

When a child feels sad, hurt, or angry, it's hard to be joyful. Help turn the frown upside down to a smile with thanksgiving statements. Let your daughter echo the words.

- I'm thankful God gave me you.

- I'm thankful for our home, food, and God's love.

- I'm thankful even when I feel sick because I trust God cares for me.

- I'm thankful for good memories.

Joy Parade or Dance

Encourage your daughter to move with joy to music. Turn it into a parade around the house. Praise God with your daughter for each body part as you move. Wiggle and shake that body part. Praise God as you travel from every part of your house, inside and out. Praise God for every member of your family. Praise God for friends.

Wear princess crowns and dress up. Use bells, musical instruments, or kitchen-band instruments. Take photos. Take turns shouting a reason to praise God, and let everyone follow it with a phrase like "God is awesome!" or "Hooray for God our King!"

Creative Prompts

Give your daughter prompts to get her creative juices flowing.

- Tell the start of a story.

- Discover an imaginative connection to a Scripture verse. For example, read the parable of the sower and ask what your daughter would plant. Then ask what she would plant in her heart.

- Describe a problem and ask for possible solutions.

- Imagine a new creature.

- Encourage your daughter to use animals, toys, and items from nature to make centerpieces.

- Read a Scripture passage and encourage her to make up a song or cheer based on the words or meaning.

- Find something good in the middle of a bad day or tough time.

Joyful Words That Inspire

Use words that affirm your daughter's creative efforts and avoid ones that crush her spirit. Great choices include the following:

- Thanks for helping me!
- I love having you help me.
- What amazing colors you chose!
- What a great idea.
- You did it!

Dad and Daughter Activities

Photo Ops

Take photos or record joyful times when you do something together.

- Watch the stars.
- Bake cookies.
- Make popcorn.
- Go for a walk.
- Examine leaves.
- Blow bubbles.
- Make a time capsule.
- Make ice cream sundaes.
- Read.

- Create fun with sidewalk chalk.
- Sing.

Bring a SMILE to Your Daughter's Face Daily

S is for *share*.

- Share interesting facts.
- Share fun by playing together (games, building blocks, going for a walk).
- Share time with her.
- Share laughter with jokes, bubbles, and whatever makes her giggle.

M is for *man up*. Be the special man in her life and a good model.

- Let her see you make repairs, check the car, and make sure things are safe.
- Be a gentleman in your words.
- Be faithful with church and reading the Bible.
- Be respectful when shopping, driving, and at home.

I is for *inspire her*.

- Compliment her character.
- Celebrate her successes.
- Cheer her on to persevere in something she is trying to learn.

L is for *listen*.

- Ask about her dreams.

- Ask about tomorrow's plans.

- Ask about her prayers.

E is for *express love.*

- Hug her and let her sit on your lap.

- Pray with her.

- Hold her.

Mom's Tools

Inspirational Activities

Inspire and sprinkle joy into a girl's life and promote creativity with some of these ideas:

- Go for a walk in a park.

- Try a new art kit.

- Modify a favorite recipe, like making a new cookie.

- Read a book and stop before the climax to ask what might happen.

- Discuss another way a story could have ended.

- Provide empty boxes, blocks, dress-up clothes, puppets, and puzzles for play.

- Allow playtime without filling her days with planned activities or lessons.

- Challenge her to create music from outdoor objects like rocks and sticks.

- Try science experiments.

- Visit museums and window shop.

Wall Art

- Hang an empty frame on a washable wall and let her watercolor inside the frame. Wash it off after a few weeks so she can make a new picture.

- Hang a frame with easel paper in it, and change out the paper when it runs out.

- Paint a wall with magnetic paint. Let her draw or cut out pictures from magazines. Add magnets to the back of the pictures, and let her use the wall as a storyboard.

- Cover a wall with flannel and give her felt shapes to use as a flannel board for creating art or stories.

Imagination Box or Station

Give your daughter a box of art supplies appropriate for her age (nothing too small for younger children). It might include glue, crayons, paint, paper, ribbon, stickers, glitter pens, scissors, yarn, straws, beads (appropriate sizes for her age), a stapler, chenille stems, tissue paper, and recycled materials. Add other items around the house or find special treasures at a craft store.

Add a few craft books that use the supplies you have to spark ideas. Creativity is built upon skills learned. For example, once a girl discovers how to make a pom-pom snowman, it's easy to start imagining other pom-pom creatures to make.

Joy and Personalities

Discover the motivation that brings daughters joy and the desire to impart joy to others.

A *Social Butterfly* loves to make others smile. She loves attention and parties.

- Locate an elderly neighbor, and send your daughter over just to chat or to give a hug.
- Make cookies together, then let your daughter serve them to guests with a smile.
- When going to the store, encourage your daughter to smile at someone who looks unhappy.
- Hold praise parties to sing and shout praises to God.

A *Born Leader* finds joy in leading, meeting goals, and having good followers.

- Put her in full charge of finding someone in the neighborhood or church who needs to be encouraged.
- Have her gather family or friends together to write a group Get Well or Happy Birthday card.
- Ask her to organize the gift giving. Encourage her to be the first to smile and present the gift.
- Encourage your daughter to keep a praise journal to record God's answers.

A *Princess of Order* finds joy in organizing and completing tasks or playing with a few close friends.

- Have her coordinate the supplies (organizing the paper, crayons, and craft paper) to create a card or gift a group will give to someone who needs a splash of joy. Let her create the basket or envelope to hold the cards. Allow her to plan when it will be taken to that person.

- Plan a playdate with one or two close friends.
- Create a quiet spot where your daughter can sit and talk to Jesus.

Everyone's Friend finds joy in relaxing with friends.

- Encourage her sense of humor by holding a joke-telling session.
- Provide an opportunity to share publicly (over dinner) what makes her joyful.
- Help her find someone who needs a faithful friend and become that person's pal.
- Find praise music your child enjoys, and encourage her to listen or sing along.

Go for Joy, Princess!

Help your child follow dreams by encouraging her to go and do things that are good for her.

1. Go outdoors and look at the wonderful world God has made. Then go draw a picture or make something beautiful.
2. Go and make a new friend. You'll have a bigger world of friends.
3. Go and talk to God. You'll find out He loves you very much.
4. Go fill your brain. Learn at school, from books, and from listening to people.
5. Go find and read books about things you like. You'll discover more interests.
6. Go listen to God. Obey what He tells you in the Bible. You'll discover His plans for you.

7. Go and use your body. Exercise. Run, jump, and play to build your muscles and relax your brain.

8. Go and eat well. Choose foods that are good for your body. That will help you think, too!

9. Go to sleep on time. Rest helps you grow and helps you look your princess best. That's why it's called *beauty sleep*.

10. Go and dream of what you can be when you grow up, and what you can learn to do. You'll find there are lots of choices.

Spurring your daughter on to fulfill her goals starts with cheering her on as she takes her first steps; then it will be her first day of school. You can see where this is going. Right now, be the first person, whenever possible, to encourage her in her firsts, which will become joy-filled moments for both of you.

Your belief in your daughter will inspire her and bring great joy to her heart.

Dad's Toolbox

Chad had a creative mind and would often make sketches of what he imagined he'd build for his clients or our girls. I remember the sketch of a toy box he wanted to build for Brandy when we didn't have the funds for Christmas gifts the year she turned two. He was inspired after he finished his sketch and began building. Upon completion, he placed her new toy box by the Christmas tree with a great sense of satisfaction. It was a beautiful, sturdy piece of furniture that was a joy for my girls and me for many years.

As my girls got older, they often spent time in Chad's shop

learning to use his tools. He worked beside them to create "dreams come true." For Kamy it was a cradle for her Cabbage Patch doll. For Brandy it was an erupting volcano for a school project that won first prize. Today both girls joyfully possess some of their dad's tools. Brandy recently built some beautiful shelves for both of her daughters' rooms. Kamy has taken over the "honey do" list of things to do around our home, just as Chad did. They loved learning from their dad and now fix and build things using his same tools.

And lead us not into temptation, but deliver us some email.

FOUR-YEAR-OLD GIRL, misquoting the Lord's Prayer on rinkworks.com

The Fruit of Goodness in Your Princess's Life

La Belle Jardinière continues to nurture a young plant by weeding and adding nutrients.

Nurturing Mother
Princess Attribute—Noble character
Fruit of the Spirit—Goodness

A BABY DOES NOT COME equipped with a noble character, but it can develop over time with proper nurturing. As a child experiences life with parents who selflessly put the child's needs and the needs of others first, noble character can grow. Children generally are wired to imitate parents who value and treat their families with love.

A mother nurtures goodness by helping her children understand right from wrong and teaching them to make good choices. A daughter grows the fruit of goodness as she serves and cares for others. See how this occurred in the life of Amy, a young girl who showed unusual goodness at an early age.

Amy: Making Friends Smile

From the time Mary Wills first expected her little girl, she sang to her and taught her about Jesus. As Amy grew, Mary told her about how Jesus wants us to care for others and to develop virtues. Together they enjoyed the character Charity Church Mouse, who sang about being a servant to all and making good choices. When friends left Amy out, or when she faced a new setting, she felt awkward or sad. That gave her the desire to make sure her friends always felt wanted. If one of Amy's friends was sick, Mary prayed for the friend with Amy and talked about an action they could take to make the friend feel better. She praised Amy when she saw her give a friend the first turn, or share her toys, or pay a compliment.

When Amy was almost eight, Mary watched Amy tote around a small notebook and apparently interview her friends. She asked her about it, and she discovered that Amy kept notes about what her friends liked or about their special needs, such as allergies. She wanted to be sure to plan fun every time she invited a friend to visit. It warmed Mary's heart to see such goodness in her daughter.

As they planned her eighth birthday party, Amy even interviewed the mother of a friend who had a milk allergy. She asked how to make cupcakes, cookies, and frosting without milk. Mary and Amy used milk and butter substitutes, setting up a station for decorating with sprinkles, frosting, and little candies. Amy planned activities where no one would feel left out or hurt, including a craft using Popsicle sticks, glitter, and sequins. Amy played hostess at her own party, making sure to welcome every guest and noticing if anyone looked like she felt awkward.

Mary asked, "Amy, are you having a good time? It's your birthday."

Amy smiled. "Oh yes, Mommy." She loved watching friends laugh and smile.

One of the mothers mentioned how much she appreciated Amy's friendship with her daughter and that she saw so many great character traits in her. She always spoke thoughtfully, shared well, and had a pleasant, positive attitude. Mary smiled and thanked God for her daughter's fruit of goodness.

Amy's noble character continued to grow with her mother's encouragement. When a friend injured her tongue and got stitches, Amy visited her. She understood the swollen tongue prevented her friend from talking or eating anything but smoothies. Amy chatted with her mother about what to do for her friend, and her mom suggested a way to communicate. So Amy made a smoothie with raspberries, her friend's favorite fruit. She brought a little tablet to "talk" with her pal, enabling the injured girl to answer questions by pointing to words on the tablet. She quickly brought smiles to her friend's face, and they giggled back and forth.

Mary loved the way her daughter cared about serving her friends, making them feel comfortable, and finding practical ways to share joy and friendship. At the same time, Amy saw her mother's actions as she cared for others and paused to pray with friends in need.

Mary knew Amy disliked feeling awkward and worked to help those around her relax and be happy. She said that whenever Amy led or invited friends over, "she always wanted everyone to feel comfortable and welcomed." She smiled at store clerks and remembered to say thanks to anyone who served her. Mary and Amy studied Proverbs 31 to discover God's description of a royal princess. Amy followed that role model and looked for ways to help family, friends, coworkers, and those she encountered.

How to Be a Nurturing Mom

We invest countless hours helping our daughters learn to dress, brush their teeth, and develop fine and gross motor skills. And, like Mary, we also invest time nurturing their character. We start by teaching manners and polite words such as *please* and *thank you*. Each step helps develop goodness. For instance, as a little girl learns to share a toy, she begins to develop a generous spirit. Our goal is that our daughters become women of noble character.

What does it mean to become a nurturing mother? To nurture is to help the growth or development of a child, to train, educate, and provide the care and attention a young child needs.

Think of times you spent with your daughter praying together, baking cookies, or enjoying a tea party while practicing appropriate manners. Remember moments you caught your daughter being a delightful princess as she shared toys, obeyed quickly, or noticed that you felt tired. Those are precious moments to cherish as you realize how you are nurturing your daughter to become a noble princess, one who is equipped for the future.

I (Karen) still struggle with living up to the description

of the noble woman of Proverbs 31, and I sometimes berate myself for my shortcomings. I know when my mother or one of my grandmothers praised me for sharing, helping with projects for the poor, or other actions that reflected goodness, it warmed my heart and brought a smile to my face. I felt like I was becoming a lady. Likewise, we fill our daughters' hearts when we teach them to help others, or praise them for their efforts and positive character traits. How God must rejoice and notice when we raise up daughters He can call noble, worthy, and more precious than rubies!

The character traits in Proverbs 31 became my own goals as well as what I desired for my daughters to achieve. I searched for specific instances when I could praise my girls for their generosity, integrity, loyalty, persistence, or another noble trait. I noticed when they gave someone a true compliment, offered to help give away more clothes and toys after a major hurricane, and worked hard to improve their grades and homemaking skills. I smiled when I saw them bake cookies for their brothers or help their dad make popcorn. I cringed when I heard them spout off angry words or selfishly not share a toy. Then I would have to have a heart-to-heart chat about the behavior and ask if that was how a lady behaved. We would decide on the best way to apologize and plan to make amends. Sometimes I would hear them parrot my more selfish phrases, and I'd realize again that I needed to nurture in myself what I wanted to grow in my daughters.

It became a nightly habit to reflect on my own actions and words. If I realized I yelled too much at my children, or only scolded them without noticing their obedience and good traits, I determined to start the next morning with an apology and a praise.

I loved how my friend Mary nurtured her daughter's character. Mary became my prayer partner, and we shared from our hearts the desire to raise our daughters to be women of faith with noble character. I followed Mary's example, using story characters as reminders to develop virtues.

The Proverbs 31 woman reminded me of various directions in which to guide and nurture my girls. I needed to make sure they grew strong physically and exercised regularly. One liked swimming, so I drove her to practices. Her dad, Jim, became a referee so he could be involved. One liked music and dance, so we enrolled her in dance lessons.

I taught my daughters homemaking skills and rejoiced when they cooked and served a meal. We bought beautiful bedcoverings and made a game of tidying our rooms. I also wanted to consider the future and their career choices, so I praised them for working hard to earn good grades. I sought ways to develop their compassion, including making sandwiches for the homeless, collecting canned goods for food pantries, and helping with children's church. Finding opportunities to exercise goodness nurtured their nobility.

Observe your daughter and find the right actions to praise. Notice the little negative actions to gently weed out with those heart-to-heart chats. Look for opportunities that meet your child's bent as you exercise her gifts and nurture her character.

Mary and I are now praying for our granddaughters and rejoicing in our grown daughters as we see them exhibiting the spiritual fruit we nurtured from their births. May God bless you with a prayer partner, possibly the mother of one of your daughter's friends, who also desires to raise a noble Modern-Day Princess.

Princess of Goodness

I (Karen) recall hearing one of my children imitate me—right down to the tone and inflection—by yelling, "Clean up this mess!" Thankfully children also imitate our good habits. One of the best ways to develop goodness in our daughters is to pause before acting or speaking. Pray and make good decisions. Our goodness, or lack of it, influences our girls. Naomi's story reveals how a daughter lived out the legacy of goodness and noble character passed along by her mother.

Naomi's Goodness

Mary's daughter Amy grew up, married, and had children of her own. Naomi, especially, seems to be a mirror image of her mother in the way she cares for others. At her fourth birthday party, Naomi paired girls together and made sure she welcomed each one. But that left her without a partner. When asked if she was okay alone, Naomi responded that seeing her friends happy made her happy—and that was her best present. She continued to make sure everyone had fun. She said she enjoyed being the hostess.

Naomi strives for peace among her friends and in her heart. She even squeezes a stress block when she feels over-whelmed. She's artistic, writes praise songs, and keeps a note-book too. Her mind is creative, and she's always imagining things to do, including what to do for others.

It's amazing to see the legacy within a family. Mary's desire to raise a noble daughter brought about a natural progression as Amy also raised a noble daughter who exhibits the fruit of goodness. When we strive to produce fruit in our daughters, it will carry over into the next generation.

Developing the Fruit of Goodness

Here's how one of my dictionaries defines the word *noble*: Belonging to a hereditary class (position of inheritance), high-born, titled. Showing fine personal qualities or high moral principles: virtuous, good, honorable, upright, decent, worthy, moral, ethical, reputable.

As the founder of Modern-Day Princess Headquarters, I (Doreen) am humbled, yet excited, to address this topic that proclaims royalty! Did your heart also leap to see that the definition so clearly equates the characteristic of being noble with the biblical definition of "belonging to a hereditary class"?

We are adopted into the royal family of God when we embrace His truth and come to know Jesus Christ as our personal Savior. Isn't it thrilling to realize we possess the greatest heritage anyone can have? Just think, we are of the highest nobility in heaven and on earth. We are highborn in God's kingdom.

We are daughters of the King. First Peter 2:9 declares: "For you have been chosen by God himself—you are priests of the King, you are holy and pure, you are God's very own—all this so that you may show to others how God called you out of the darkness into his wonderful light" (TLB). Our royal heritage comes with an equally significant call to high moral principles by its association with God our King, who is perfect and holy.

Did you notice that the word *good*—the root of *goodness*, a fruit of the Spirit—is listed right in the definition of *noble*? How often over the years did I repeat this favorite phrase of my mom's to my daughters: "Let's be a good girl, okay?" It's a common phrase used among moms because they desire their offspring to be well-behaved. It's important because our behavior reveals our goodness. It's music to a mother's ears when someone says, "Oh, I just have to tell you that your daughter was such a good (delightful, helpful, courteous, etc.) girl today." You feel like all those times you imparted correction or encouragement made an impact.

Goodness is highly noticed across the world. For example, "good" women who have made a difference through history include Mother Teresa, Florence Nightingale, and Corrie ten Boom. Their goodness shone through their actions, and they became worthy of being titled honorable, upright, decent, worthy, moral, and reputable—all synonyms of *noble*!

Developing goodness requires consistent parenting. Whenever possible we should acknowledge each time our little princesses do something notably good. Whether through word or deed, our praise will motivate them to repeat those actions. Have you found that to be true? Reflect for a moment and remember what made you feel excited about doing something good when you were a little girl.

I remember an important character quality that my parents wanted to see in my life. They encouraged me to be quiet when adults talked. I remember one evening my parents invited some friends over for a visit. Upon their departure, my mother turned to me and said, "What a good girl you were this evening. You stayed quiet while the adults chatted." I grinned with delight because she noticed I had accomplished something big for me. I respected her wishes and controlled myself. Her words provided a powerful affirmation as I developed the fruit of goodness.

I encourage you to find opportunities to impart words of encouragement often to your princess. Also encourage family members and friends. Make a simple phone call to thank a parent or relative, text a friend who blessed you, or call a cousin whose goodness made a difference in your life. Remember your princess is watching you and will base her actions on what she sees modeled for her.

Inspiring goodness doesn't have to be a big or contrived effort. I am praying we will live out 1 Timothy 5:10 as we each build a reputation for good deeds; become women who bring up children well; receive strangers in our homes; perform humble duties for other Christians; help people in trouble; and devote ourselves to doing good.

I am cheering you on to goodness that reveals your nobility and that of your daughter.

Fruitful Activities

Fruit of the Spirit Verse

"A wife of noble character who can find? She is worth far more than rubies" (Proverbs 31:10, NIV). Proverbs 31 serves as a guide for setting goals to become women of noble character. Remember that a noble princess produces goodness.

The Greek word for "goodness" is *agathosune*, which

means to aggressively seek excellence. It also includes the idea of having the strength to produce good results.

Goodness also confirms that something has fulfilled its purpose. For example, when God completed each day of Creation, He said it was *good*. Expressions of goodness are acts that reach out to benefit or bless others.

Treasure Box Addition

Talk about growing up and becoming God's precious princess worth more than rubies. Place a red bauble in the treasure box as a reminder to make good choices, just like the Proverbs 31 daughter of the King.

Spa Time for Body Goodness

Connect the good of caring for your body to the goodness of caring for people. It's important to be clean inside and out, and even in your mind and heart. That's part of being noble and excellent. Enjoy the fun of a foot-spa time of washing, massaging, and anointing your daughter's feet and painting her toes. Let her wash your feet too. Talk about choosing what is good for others and walking away from sin. Chat about purity and guarding her body.

Enjoy the following activities and use them as object lessons to reinforce this point.

- *Minty Princess Foot Scrub*: Whisk three tablespoons white sugar and six tablespoons of brown sugar. Add two tablespoons olive oil and one and one-half teaspoons of mint extract. Wash your feet and pat dry, leaving them damp. Rub on the scrub and massage as long as desired. Wash off.

- *Princess Glow*: Sprinkle cosmetic body glitter into a mix of two teaspoons aloe vera gel and one-half of a teaspoon nonpetroleum jelly to make a sparkling gel to rub on your feet or face. It's good for skin and adds a glowing shimmer. The aloe and nonpetroleum jelly are also good for your skin to soothe and protect as well as moisturize it.

- *Princess Sparkle Dust*: Mix cosmetic body glitter into powder to make princess dust to add sparkle to her skin.

- *Water, Water Every Day*: Talk about the importance of drinking water for healthy skin and hair and even brighter-looking eyes. Water also helps build better muscle tone. Make the water sweeter by adding a piece of fruit or sprig of mint.

Good Deeds

Each day, think of a good deed you can do with your daughter. It might be as simple as making her brother's bed, baking cookies for a sick friend, or donating canned goods to a food drive.

Goodness Album

Help your daughter make a booklet or album of pictures that reflect goodness.

- Make a page for each day of Creation.
- Add pictures of good deeds, such as playing well with friends or doing chores.
- Add photos or drawings of reading the Bible, going to church, and praying.

Be an Encouraging Goose!

Canadian geese are known for their cooperative spirit as they fly in formation to reduce wind resistance. Keep a stuffed goose in the house to honk encouragement as a reminder when you pass by it. As a mother and daughter, follow the example of the geese:

- Geese honk to encourage one another. Honk and shout praises.

- Geese are loyal and mate for life. Be loyal.

- When a goose is hurt and falls from the sky, two others fly to remain with the hurt one. They care for the goose, bringing food and nursing it.

- Geese fly in a V shape that actually uses the wind to help them all fly with less effort. Be the wind beneath the wings of others through your support.

Sparkling Jar of Goodness

Let your daughter help you mix up some simple ingredients and add sparkly items to make this container that glitters. Shake it as a way to celebrate good deeds.

You will need:

- Rubbing alcohol
- Empty clear jar and screw-on lid, like a small plastic peanut butter jar
- Vegetable oil
- Shiny tiny objects like beads, sequins, and glitter
- Tape

Follow these steps to complete this fun project:

1. Pour rubbing alcohol in jar until one-quarter filled.
2. Add vegetable oil, leaving about half an inch of air at the top, and let it settle to the bottom.

3. Drop objects into the liquids.

4. Fill jar to brim with more oil.

5. Screw on lid and tape it closed.

6. Watch what happens when you shake the jar. It adds sparkle and twinkles. The objects dance.

Talk about how goodness and helpful deeds add sparkle to our lives as we dance for God. Every day your princess performs good deeds or shows good character, shake the jar and dance while the items dance in the jar.

Dad and Daughter Activities

Compliments Fit for a Princess

Dad, share compliments in the following areas to enhance your daughter's self-esteem:

- inner beauty
- modesty
- courage
- persistence
- talents or skills

Reward Her Noble Character

Give your daughter a special red necklace to represent a ruby. Use it to affirm her when you see her developing the fruit of the Spirit. Talk with her about how you see her growing into a woman such as the one described in Proverbs 31.

Measuring Pole

Find a pole with which to measure your daughter. Each time you measure her height, talk about how she is growing her character at the same time she is growing taller. Point out a positive character trait you've seen in her, such as goodness.

Mom's Tools

Gardening Activity

Plant a little indoor or outdoor garden with your daughter, and use it as a springboard to talk about how to grow into a noble lady.

- Choose seeds together. You can plant anything from a small herb garden to a big vegetable or flower garden. Each princess is unique, just as gardens are unique.

- Dig into the soil and remove rocks and stones. Point out that pulling out obstacles in the soil is similar to the way we need to remove sin in our lives for healthy growth.

- Plant the seeds. Explain that in our hearts we need to plant virtues, such as respect.

- Let the sun shine on the soil, and add water as needed. Mention the way praise and love help our character grow.

- Remove weeds that pop up. Explain that in our lives, we must continually be on the lookout for the "weeds" of sin and disobedience.

- Watch the seeds sprout, grow, and bloom. Talk about how your princess continues to grow and bloom.

Good Choices and Teachable Moments

At the end of each day of Creation, God looked at what He did and saw it was good. Use this chart to help your princess look at her day to see what was good. Chat about choices made and use less-than-good incidents as teachable moments to share what better or other choices could have been made.

What I Did	Was It Good?
Foods I ate	
Exercise	
Obeying rules	
Telling the truth	
Choices I made	
Helping others	
Prayers	
Bible reading or devotion	
Bedtime	
Morning time and going to school	

Proverbs 31 Princess

Someday your Modern-Day Princess will become a woman. Guide her character to be a noble one by helping her strive along with you to be Proverbs 31 princesses. Try some of these princess actions to develop noble character.

Princess Character	Verse	Princess Action
Trustworthy, loyal	11	Keep your promises, and do your chores without reminders.
Hard worker who follows through (diligent)	13	Help with household chores like dusting, sweeping, clearing the table, doing dishes, laundry.
Thrifty (wise with money)	16	Make good choices with money, give some to your church, save some.
Physically fit	17	Exercise.
Industrious, makes things	19	Make gifts and cards to give others.
Compassionate and generous	20	Give away clothes and toys to the poor, or canned food to a food pantry.
Responsible	22	Take care of your clothes and put them away.
Graceful and confident	25	Walk gracefully and believe in yourself.
Thoughtful (speaks wisely)	26	Think before you speak and be kind with your words; share the gospel; and compliment others.
Focused with purpose (helps care for her family and is not lazy)	27	Make snacks for family members, spend time keeping your room neat.
Humbly fears the Lord	30	Pray and remember that God is awesome!

Goodness and Personality

Help your child in her natural bent to develop good character and overcome weaknesses.

A *Social Butterfly* loves praise when she's good.

- Your daughter naturally likes to cheer people up. Praise her for being a cheerleader.

- Remind her to give other people turns and to let others have the spotlight.

- Reward her for following through and keeping promises.

A *Born Leader* will be motivated to goodness if it is stated as a goal.

- Remind your daughter to find the good in everyone and to encourage others.

- Praise her for meeting her goals and working hard.

- Remind her to be thoughtful and thank people.

A *Princess of Order* works hard to be good and noble.

- Praise her work ethic and neatness.

- Overcome whining with praise such as "I'm glad for rain because it waters the plants." Or "I am thankful that it's just a cut and not worse. The ouch will go away."

- Remind her to share generously.

Everyone's Friend can build on her natural desire for peace and making others feel at ease.

- Praise her generosity and ability to share.

- Reward her when she works and completes a task.

- Remind her to be responsible with keeping things organized.

Dad's Toolbox

An important item in any toolbox is a measuring tape. It measures the height, width, and depth of any project. It is used to make the end product look good from every side. It prevents errors and maintains accuracy so the work turns out true. My dad repaired many chairs over the years and depended on his measuring tape. We could trust his chairs to hold us because of his integrity as a woodworker who used excellent measurements.

Our heavenly Father, in His goodness, provides in His Word a true gauge (the measuring tape) for noble character: "O LORD, who may abide in Your tent? Who may dwell on Your holy hill? He who walks with integrity, and works righteousness, and speaks truth in his heart. He does not slander with his tongue, nor does evil to his neighbor, nor takes up a reproach against his friend; In whose eyes a reprobate is despised, but who honors those who fear the LORD; He swears to his own hurt and does not change; He does not put out his money at interest, nor does he take a bribe against the innocent. He who does these things will never be shaken" (Psalm 15:1-5, NASB).

A dad, using his measuring tape of goodness, will be a man of noble character who models goodness for his daughter.

"I'm never having kids.
I hear they take nine months to download."

LITTLE GIRL, quoted on broadcaster.org

The Fruit of Gentleness in Your Princess's Life

La Belle Jardinière cultivates plants by
pruning them, cutting off the dead ends, and
trimming them for maximum growth.

Cultivating Mothers
Princess Attribute—Compassion
Fruit of the Spirit—Gentleness

AS MOTHERS WE STRIVE consistently to cultivate (to develop) our little princesses to become "good little girls."

I (Doreen) remember one of my daughters telling me that she watched how mean her friend was when her little brother fell and scraped his knee just as they headed outside. Her friend yelled, "Oh, just get up. We've got to go to my friend's house right now, and you are going to make me late!" Did you feel the "Ouch!" in your heart as you read those words?

Her words clearly demonstrated a lack of the fruit of gentleness. I cheer you on today to persevere as you cultivate this fruit in your daughter's life. Continue to encourage compassion so you will see the beautiful fruit of gentleness grow.

Kamy's Gentle Heart

I (Doreen) and the rest of my family, rejoiced with delight when Muffin, our sweet golden retriever, was expecting her first litter of pups. Our expectation grew as her time to deliver got closer. One early morning I awoke to find she had already given birth to three precious puppies. Chad, the girls, and I all hovered in the laundry room to watch Muffin deliver six more pups. She seemed to have no objections to our presence around her. She was a natural at being a mom for the first time. We enjoyed watching her begin to nurse the puppies throughout the day, and we all slept peacefully that night knowing she was doing well.

Unfortunately, the following morning Kamy came running into our bedroom and yelled, "One of the puppies is dead, Mommy. One of the puppies is dead!" I immediately rushed in to see for myself. Sure enough, one of the puppies had not made it through the night. Once Kamy got past her tears, she felt angry toward Muffin. She thought the puppy died because Muffin had pushed its little body away from her and the other puppies that were feeding. I wrapped my arms around Kamy and just let her cry.

When her crying subsided to a whimper, I told her that God gives animals the ability to know things. Muffin knew one of her puppies was dying, and she needed to keep the other eight alive by feeding them. That's why she gently pushed the dead pup to the side. I shared with her how I was sad too (which I truly was) seeing that precious little pup now cold and lifeless. I held her close, not knowing myself why God allows little people or puppies to die untimely deaths.

But I reassured Kamy—and myself—that we can trust Him. He says in His Word that He even knows when a sparrow falls to the ground (Matthew 10:29). It was a solemn day for both of us as we grieved.

The next day, I saw Kamy gently petting Muffin and taking time to hold every one of the puppies before and after school. I had never seen such compassion in my six-year-old until this very painful experience.

Not long after the puppy died, the kids on the bus started to tease Brandy quite harshly. After several days of this, Kamy came to me, crying because she felt so angry with those kids who were mean to her big sister. She confessed that she told those kids to "shut up!" That was not an acceptable phrase in our household, but she couldn't help herself because she hurt so much for her sister. Once again, I saw her spirit of compassion. I explained that when our hearts are hurt it is easy to get angry, and we want to hurt whoever is dishing out that pain. The Lord brought to my mind the verse about how we are not to return evil for evil (see 1 Peter 3:9).

As an adult today, Kamy is known in our family as the compassionate one. She is always the first to come to the aid of an animal or person who is hurting. God has used this gift to bless others through Kamy as she reveals one of God's greatest gifts to us: compassion.

How to Be a Mom Who Cultivates Compassion

As moms, our gentleness will help cultivate compassion in our daughters. Our kind words or actions toward others will enable them to see how others respond to comfort and reassurance. Furthermore, nothing delights a mother's heart more than seeing her daughter demonstrate compassion as she speaks gently and echoes her mother's comforting words (perhaps to her dolls when she is very young). Soon she'll show compassion to a sibling or a little friend. Oh, the joy of seeing the fruit of your labor!

A dictionary definition of *cultivate* is to grow or raise something under conditions that you can control. The word also encompasses the idea of improving something through diligent labor, care, study, or encouragement.

Have you ever seen yourself as a "cultivator" of gentleness and compassion in your daughter's life?

As I (Doreen) read the definition for the word *cultivate* today, I remembered my own parenting years and speaking some of those words, seeking to live them out. I didn't always cultivate gentleness perfectly, but I was trying. Early on I knew the importance of fulfilling my call to raise up my daughters in the way that they should go, so that they would not depart from it when they were old (see Proverbs 22:6).

When I saw an unhealthy, self-destructive behavior in one of my girls, I *studied* her over a short period of time to understand the root of her actions. Other times I found myself *refining* her etiquette. Last but not least, I *encouraged* each of my girls in her God-given artistic and musical gifts. Wow! A moment of reflection showed that I *was* a cultivator, just as you are.

Today, my girls are cultivating me when it comes to technology. They show me how to download music on my cell phone, back up a TV show when I miss the last five minutes, or upload a document to my iPad. How wonderful that cultivation works both ways!

Cultivation requires us to also embrace stronger words—words such as *control* and *labor*. Both words instantly make me feel tired. Control? I remember thinking at times, *What or who do I really ever have under control, especially once my girls started walking or talking?* I was so excited to see them grow, but quickly experienced lack of control in getting them not to talk to me when I was on the phone or not to touch the breakables on my knickknack shelf.

One day I asked advice from my wonderful friend and mentor, Emilie Horner, who had two children, ages five and seven. As a novice, I admired her experienced parenting, because my girls were only two and four. One of the first things Emilie firmly proclaimed? "This is going to require some labor to establish your control."

I wasn't excited to hear that news. It made me a bit fearful. However, she began sharing helpful tips in raising my precious, yet curious and mischievous, little princesses. One piece of sage advice was "Don't put everything away that you don't want them to touch. Leave several unbreakable items on a shelf." She said to instruct the children not to touch these items. This provided an opportunity for them to learn obedience without the parent being fearful or angry about breaking something of value. What great advice!

I placed some unbreakable items on the bottom knickknack shelf. I instructed the girls that if they didn't touch the shelf by nap time, they would receive a reward—getting a cookie or going to the park. Oh, the temptation remained great because the "untouchables" sat within reach of their little hands. And yes, they did pick them up and tote them off.

When I discovered an unbreakable vase or figurine had

disappeared, I followed Emilie's advice. I asked where they put it, then sent them to find it and return it to its rightful place. They already knew the consequence—no cookie or trip to the park. In turn, I began to gain a level of control. Or should I say that I learned I had the power to influence and cultivate my girls' behavior in a constructive manner?

As the girls successfully learned not to touch the unbreakable knickknacks, they gained the privilege of touching the more highly valued items. This training helped them handle fragile items with gentleness.

I pray that you have an "Emilie" in your life. You could be blessed with a mom, a mother-in-law, a sister, a seasoned friend, or a mentor to call upon in those moments when you need a little wisdom. Look for someone who will encourage and guide you in cultivating the fruit of gentleness, or any other fruit of the Spirit, in your princess or princesses.

Princess of Gentleness

From the moment you first hold your baby, she feels your touch. She knows when you are gently caressing her or firmly burping her. Gentleness requires a balance of being firm and tender. When burping a baby, it's important to pat him or her firmly. If the pat is too soft, it won't effectively release air bubbles. Of course, we show young children how a baby or animal needs to be touched very softly. Children experiment with touch as they try to understand how gentle is really gentle.

The following story describes how one little girl used her knowledge of gentleness to help in an emergency.

Gentle Hands

"Mommy! Michael's hand is bleeding!" Rebecca yelled as she dashed up the stairs. I (Karen) grabbed a towel, raced downstairs, and wrapped Michael's hand in the towel. He'd had an accident working with my husband, who hadn't noticed because of the noise of the power tools they were working with. So I applied pressure to stop the bleeding. I yanked the plug on my husband's power sander to stop the noise and said, "Michael is bleeding. He got hurt working with you and ran off."

Michael had sanded off a fingernail. The continued bleeding meant a trip to the emergency room, but I needed to stay home with our younger children.

I showed Rebecca how to hold up Michael's arm while she pressed on his thumb at a pressure point below the knuckle. As my husband and I buckled their seat belts, I told Rebecca, "Don't let go of Michael's thumb until an adult takes over."

Then I added, "Be gentle, but firm. You want to stop the bleeding but not cut off the circulation."

My husband stopped in front of the emergency room to let the children out. Rebecca walked in holding up Michael's arm. A medic pointed them out to everyone in the waiting room. He said, "Everyone look. This is the first person this week who knew how to treat someone bleeding, and she's only a child."

He asked Rebecca, "How did you know what to do?"

She meekly replied, "My mommy told me to keep his arm up and press here until an adult takes Michael's thumb. My arm's tired. Can you hold Michael's thumb now?"

He laughed, took Michael, and said, "You have a smart mom, and you listen well."

Later, Rebecca asked what I meant by being "gentle but firm." I explained that it meant to use her strength but to control it so she wouldn't stop the blood from moving in his hand. I showed her how to tell if there was a pulse and mentioned that stopping bleeding needs to be gentle enough to let the pulse continue. If the tip of Michael's thumb had turned blue, it would have shown she pressed too hard and cut off the blood flow inside his vein.

As we talked, I affirmed her heart as well as her actions. I said that her honesty in admitting she didn't know first aid showed that she was humble and gentle in spirit.

Cultivating the Fruit of Gentleness

Cultivate gentleness by developing a sense of compassion in your Modern-Day Princess. Chat about the importance of knowing when to be gentle and when to be stronger. A girl can play soccer and kick the ball hard to score a goal. But if she kicks her toys, books, or a person, that hurts the person and can do damage to things. She needs to gently control her legs and feet around the house and around people.

A daughter can give her mom or dad a tight squeeze, but she needs to give a baby a light or gentle hug. Girls can be loud when cheering a team on to victory, but yelling in the house does not reflect a gentle spirit. Words to cheer the team to win are good, but unkind words that put down the other team do not reflect a gentle heart.

Beyond a gentle physical touch, the gentleness of compassion in your heart matters most. And compassion should guide a girl to touch softly and speak softly when appropriate.

It takes mindful parenting to include activities that teach gentleness and a gentle spirit. I (Karen) loved parading and dancing with my children, but I also took time to have whisper parties and sharing times of holding baby dolls gently.

I worked at teaching my children to be honest, yet not boast of their skills. Practicing humility can be hard for me, because my family invested countless hours teaching me many skills that made it easy to feel proud. I learned to ask people about themselves rather than telling them about my accomplishments. I shared with my daughters how to use questions to discover more about other people. We practiced role-playing: pretending to meet people and asking them questions to learn about someone else. We also discussed new people they met and any interesting facts they found out about new friends. That cultivated interest in people.

As we share with our girls about compassion that promotes gentleness, it's good to chat about ways to provide extra care. For example, when we took names off an Angel Tree to give clothes to the poor, we added little treasures. We put notes, money, and little toys into each pocket. We practiced first aid to show ways to gently care for people when they are hurt, such as softly covering them with a blanket to prevent shock, then adding a pillow for comfort.

Gentle touches and thoughtful actions show that we think of the other person's needs ahead of our own.

Fruitful Activities

Try activities that promote gently using our hands, voices, and hearts.

Fruit of the Spirit Verse

"Your beauty comes from inside you. It is the beauty of a gentle and quiet spirit. Beauty like this doesn't fade away. God places great value on it" (1 Peter 3:4).

Gentleness is more than using a soft voice or touch. It's also having a soft heart of compassion that feels empathy and shares in someone's sadness or pain. When a child feels pain, then comfort, she is better able to understand another's pain and the need for compassion.

Treasure Box Addition

Place a precious "breakable" figurine of a lamb inside the box as a reminder of Christ's gentleness and the truth that He is our Shepherd. A less-expensive option would be to use a white cotton ball or toy sheep.

Egg Experiments in Strength and Fragility

Guide your daughter to cradle an egg in her palm. Wrap her fingers around it and squeeze hard. Notice that it doesn't break because it is strong. Did you know that a person can even gently stand on a dozen eggs in a carton and not break any?

Help your daughter hit the egg against a bowl and nick it. It cracks open easily. The egg is also fragile. Then explain how we're like the egg. We can be strong and know that God made our hearts strong, but we also recognize that certain words and actions can nick our hearts and hurt our feelings.

Talk with your daughter about the fact that a princess is

strong but also fragile. It's important to have compassion and a spirit of gentleness to protect fragile hearts.

"Wheel" Be Gentle Paper Plate Wheel Window

Gather these supplies:

- two paper plates
- paper brad
- scissors
- crayons or markers

Make it:

1. Mark one plate into eight pie wedges. Cut one wedge out, but not too close to the edge or center. This forms a window.

2. Mark a second plate to form eight pie wedges. Inside each wedge, let your daughter draw or write about something that needs a gentle touch or compassion. Examples include: faces, babies, cuts or "owies," baby animals, new plants, hearts, friends, and china or glass.

3. Place the plate with the window over the one with the drawings.

4. Make a hole in the center, push the brad in, and fasten it. The top wheel can be turned to show one picture at a time. Turn it and talk about ways to be gentle for each item pictured.

Stuffed Animals and Dolls

Start with inanimate objects to teach gentleness. Model how to hold a baby doll, to change its diaper or clothes, and to talk to it sweetly. Show how to pet an animal, feed it, and make a comfy bed for it.

Hold a doll or stuffed-animal party. Ask every child to bring her favorite doll or animal. Let each one take a turn introducing her doll or pet and share what's special about it. Pass around the dolls or animals to give everyone a turn to hold or pet them. Cut blankets for each from polar fleece cloth.

Transfer this lesson to everyday life by visiting a petting zoo or a neighbor with a younger child and encouraging your child to care for the animal or baby gently. Take photos of your princess interacting and post the pictures as a reminder to be gentle.

First Aid

Our skin is designed to offer great protection for the fragile veins and organs inside. But sometimes skin breaks open when we get a cut. Then we need to care for the cut and stop the bleeding. Talk about first aid with your princess, and discuss how to gently care for a small wound.

1. First, stop the bleeding. Elevate the part with the cut; if needed, use gentle-but-firm pressure to stop the bleeding. Show your child pressure points and how to elevate the body part that is bleeding.

2. When the bleeding stops, gently wash the area, dry it, and add antiseptic if needed.

3. Cover it with a bandage.

4. Make the patient comfortable, letting the person lie down or sit in a comfortable chair.

Use a permanent marker to draw a heart on the bandage as a reminder that God loves His princess.

Gentle Hearts and Gentle Hands

Use some lotion on your daughter's hands to keep them soft. Have fun with a manicure while you talk about gentle touching. Touch different objects and discuss what is soft, hard, prickly, rough, etc. Talk about ways to touch living beings such as animals and people. Use a doll to demonstrate how to be gentle with a baby. Use a stuffed animal to talk about being gentle with an animal.

Dad and Daughter Activities

Show Love in Gentle Ways

There are so many ways a dad can demonstrate love and care to his daughter. Here are a few ideas to get you started:

- hugs and kisses
- cuddles
- piggyback rides
- a pat on the back
- cuddly words
- a loving squeeze
- gentle wrestling
- listening with your eyes
- whispers (but use your gentle voice to whisper messages, not secrets, such as "I love you")

Doll Play

Play with your daughter using her dolls. Show her how you held her when she was a baby. Show her how you dressed her or burped her. Look at her baby pictures. Talk about how tiny she was and how you feared breaking her, but your hands learned to be gentle.

Mom's Tools

Cultivate Empathy

It's hard for little ones to understand how other people feel. It starts with identifying their own feelings and learning words associated with emotions.

- Read books about feelings, and discuss the facial expressions in the book.

- Make faces for different emotions, and name the emotions.

- When your daughter is happy, sad, angry, etc., say what you notice. For example: "I see your smile. You look happy."

- Observe with your child how others react in order to build understanding and empathy. If your child pushed or hit another child, say something like "Look, your friend has a sad face. She is rubbing her arm where you pushed her. I see some tears on her face." Then you can guide your child to say she is sorry.

- If your child is angry, wait until she calms down, then talk about how she felt. Validate natural feelings, but correct negative reactions. "It's okay to feel mad when someone takes your toy, but it's not okay to respond by hitting her."

The Power of Two in Cultivating Compassion in Girls

Choose one accomplishment or character trait your child does well. Then choose one problem your child exhibits frequently. Focus on just those two aspects of your child's behavior for a few days or a week. Praise your child for the positive behavior and encourage her to improve the other. Coupling something well done with an area that needs improvement is less over-whelming and gives her the power to believe in her abilities and the power to improve.

Compassionate Responses

Help your princess know what actions show compassion for people, critters, and the earth:

- hugs and smiles
- kind words
- gently petting an animal
- whispers
- offering to pray for someone you know
- sending get-well cards
- congratulating someone on a good job or winning a game
- listening quietly and responding to the words and feelings shown
- a gentle pat
- making sandwiches for the homeless
- giving toys or clothes to a shelter
- getting a tired mom or dad a snack or glass of water
- walking carefully in nature
- caring for a pet
- picking up litter
- welcoming a friend who visits and letting the friend choose an activity

- giving Mom a shoulder rub after she worked hard all day
- forgiving others

Personality and Cultivating Gentleness

Help your daughter develop compassion and gentleness according to her natural bent.

A *Social Butterfly* tends to be overly demonstrative, so remind her of how others need gentleness.

- Praise your daughter for showing a welcoming spirit, and remind her to greet people with gentle hugs.
- Remind your daughter to notice how her friends feel.
- Hold a doll party for your daughter and her friends to gently care for their dolls.
- Practice using a soft voice.

A *Born Leader* wants her accomplishments noticed, walks loudly, and is not always gentle or considerate, so motivate her with goals.

- Remind your daughter to think about the feelings of others and to be considerate.
- Encourage her to list what friends need and like.
- Thank God daily for her talents and abilities to help her humbly remember where they come from.
- Practice gentle answers.

A *Princess of Order* is naturally gentle and compassionate.

- Praise your daughter for showing she cares about others and for using her gentle touch.

- Help her not to be too sensitive when others aren't gentle, but to forgive instead, as that keeps her heart tender and compassionate.
- Avoid lecturing this sensitive child.
- Let her show you how she cares for her dolls and stuffed animals.

Everyone's Friend's relaxed and diplomatic style can motivate her to be gentle.

- Read books about compassion for people in need and those who helped the needy.
- Encourage her to use natural diplomacy to keep peace and to help everyone agree.
- Remind your daughter to use her sense of humor gently and not to tease others.

Dad's Toolbox

Pliers are important tools to keep on hand. They are used to grip, position, tighten, or loosen. I remember Chad attempting to get a firm grip on some staples with a pair of needle-nose pliers to loosen and remove them from a mass-produced bookshelf that was falling apart. The key to his success in their removal was to gently pull them out so he could salvage the piece of furniture. After the air cleared from his feelings about the manufacturer, he put it back together with quality nails and glue.

I use my needle-nose pliers whenever a necklace hook needs to be replaced. Those pliers and the art of gentleness are necessary when working on a delicate chain. Over the years at home, another use for our pliers involved the occasional stubborn baby tooth that wouldn't fall out on its own. Kamy, our youngest, had lamented to her daddy one day that she had a tooth that wouldn't come out. Chad went to the garage to locate a pair of pliers, returning in her presence ready to help. She was immediately overwhelmed with fear seeing a tool that looked bigger than her little tooth. Chad immediately embraced her with a warm hug, reassuring her that he would be gentle. Trusting her daddy, she willingly opened her mouth, and he removed the loose tooth with one slight pull.

"It didn't even hurt, Daddy!" she exclaimed. He just smiled and hugged her again.

Gentleness and compassion in a dad's toolbox will help a daughter trust his strong hand.

*Children are the hands by which
we take hold of heaven.*

HENRY WARD BEECHER, reverend and social activist

The Fruit of Kindness in Your Princess's Life

*La Belle Jardinière is an encourager who puts down
mulch to protect plants from the sun's heat and
provide extra nutrients to bring about strong growth.*

Encouraging Mothers
Princess Attribute—Encourager
Fruit of the Spirit—Kindness

A SIMPLE SMILE AS you pass someone on the street reveals kindness and often brings a returned smile. Throughout my life, I (Doreen) have seen that nothing brings a smile more quickly than a word of kindness. These words can be as simple as "That's a cute scarf you are wearing," or "I hope you have a good day." I enjoy finding opportunities to encourage others.

As we model simple acts of kindness and our girls see the result, it will motivate them to do the same, because they will feel the joy that comes from encouraging and imparting kindness to others. As we praise our daughters when we hear them speak kindly, we foster the fruit of kindness. The following story suggests a simple way to encourage your daughter's kindness.

Victory's Story: The Marble Jar

Recently, one of Victory's children was struggling with her confidence as a student. One element of learning came much more easily to Victory's older daughter than it did to her youngest one. In a weak moment, with tears in her eyes, the little girl asked her mother, "Do you wish I was more like my sister?"

Victory continues the story in her own words:

As a second-born myself, my heart broke when my daughter asked that difficult question. So her daddy and I embraced this opportunity to love on her. We encouraged her as we talked about her gifts, her ability to love others, her sense of humor, and her quick wit. We were able to convince her that we truly did not want *two* of her big sister—one was quite enough!

We reassured our daughter that we treasure both of our children as unique gifts from God. We explained how imbalanced our family would be without her unique personality. It was a wonderful moment to embrace her in a personal and deliberate way as we sought to squash her fears and the comparison that so easily entangles young girls.

As moms, we may embrace our strengths, but what do we do with our weaknesses? A few years ago I became intensely aware of the fact that I am not "naturally wired" to be an encourager. I have been entrusted with four wonderful kids who deserve to hear how proud they make me. I tend to notice what needs fixing before I notice the amazing things all around me. And I recognized that is not the mom I wanted to be.

Each year, my family prays for the Lord to put a theme or word in our hearts that we can focus on throughout the next twelve months. Several years ago, we felt drawn to the fruit of the Spirit. We focused on a different "fruit" each week— talking about it, identifying what it looks like in our daily lives, defining what each means, and so forth. I wanted to encourage my children more as I saw them exercising these fruits in their daily interactions.

A friend's "marble system" inspired me to implement a version of it in our home. Each time I saw one of my children doing something with love, joy, peace, patience, kindness, goodness, gentleness, self-control, and faithfulness, I would let him or her put a marble in their jar. When they "earned" fifty marbles, they got a date with either parent, having their choice of what to do and with whom. In a big family like ours, one-on-one time can be scarce, so we all love these special activities together.

This system also provides a measurable way to recognize when I am failing to encourage them. If a few days pass with no one earning a marble, chances are I did not affirm them. They deserve my encouragement, even when it feels like we are all "works in progress" with a long way to go! The marble system causes me to ask myself what I am expecting from my children. I should never expect perfection, but I should encourage them when they make an effort. When I see evidence of the fruit of the Spirit in my children, it gives me a glimpse of what the Lord is doing in their hearts. We all need Jesus: every day, every hour, every minute.

I want to pour generously into my children, realizing I am an example of their heavenly Father who is easy to please, and who never holds back His affection from us. As I grow as an encourager with each "Great job" or "I love your enthusiasm," my children are the beneficiaries of God's gracious work in me. We are growing together as we allow the Lord to work in our hearts, revealing the fruit of His Spirit produced in us.

How to Be an Encouraging Mom

I believe that the vast majority of all moms are encouragers, powerful cheerleaders to and for their children. We can't help ourselves because we want to cheer our little girls on in each step of life, especially when fear is their initial response. Our encouragement flows from our confidence that God loves us.

As we show confidence in our daughters and support their efforts, they embrace our encouragement. Our encouragement, in turn, motivates our girls to press forward. We will rejoice in their successes and victories.

Webster's definition of the word *encourage* is this: the action of giving someone support, confidence, or hope. To inspire, motivate, fortify, persuade, cheer up, champion, or cultivate.

But before we address your role as an encouraging mom, let's talk about your own need for encouragement. *Encouragement* is one of the most frequently used words in my (Doreen's) vocabulary. Why? Because I love the results in my own life when I am encouraged. I like being inspired, cheered up, and given hope. It has motivated me to embrace the pain in my life and turn it into power. It has persuaded me to laugh at myself when I have stubbornly hung on to my selfish pride. It has cultivated my confidence to take that next bold step of faith in my life.

Have you discovered how often personal encouragement can come from God's written Word, the Bible? Oh, what joy explosions I have experienced reading my Bible over the years. It is so thrilling when the Lord speaks to me personally about a specific situation through a verse that "just happens" to be in my devotional or Bible study journal that day. Those are over-the-top personal words of inspiration from my heavenly Daddy!

Have you had that same word or verse show up through the voices of friends, family, or church members, or even in a song? Even when you hadn't shared your struggle with anyone? Did you realize that God wanted to encourage you? Sometimes encouragement may also come through a text, an e-mail, a handwritten card, or a note scribbled on the back of a bulletin and handed across the aisle in church. Don't you love when that happens? Surprises are among the best gifts of encouragement!

Our heavenly Father is the greatest Encourager of all, and He knows best how to get your attention and impart powerful, life-changing, encouraging words, especially when you need them.

Have you spoken a simple word of kindness to a stranger that turned that frown into a smile? Or did an affirmative nod of support during someone's moment of doubt inspire that person to boldly move forward? Or did you share a verse with a friend who was seeking God's direction—and it turned out your friend had just read the same verse? It's an awe-inspiring moment when you realize God has used you to encourage someone else.

Encouragement is like an investment. You can't give it without a good return. When you feel prompted to impart a word of encouragement, 99 percent of the time you will receive a smile, a thank-you, or a response such as "How did you know I needed that right now?" It truly is refreshing for you, too.

Sometimes—one percent of the time—awkward moments result after you share a sincere word of encouragement with a person who just can't receive it. It's possible that person is hurting or they just have nothing to give back. In such times it's wise to pull out all the stops and respond with a warm and understanding smile. Choose your words and moments wisely, and remember there are rewards that come from reaching out to the "one percent."

I wish I were in your presence right now and could just throw confetti as I entered your door. Then I'd spill those Valentine's Day heart candies all around you and start picking each one up, proclaiming those wonderful words that every woman and mom needs to hear: "You are so patient. You are kind. You are beautiful. You make me smile. You bring the sunshine. You are gentle. You are the apple of His eye. Thank you. I remember. I love you."

I know I can't literally do that, but I sure know that God can, will, and does affirm you through fabulous and unique messages that get your attention. So keep your eyes and ears open to receive His encouraging words that are just for you. Be ready to be His beautiful gift of encouragement to others, as you no doubt already are!

Now we're ready to talk about encouraging our little princesses.

It's natural to encourage our little ones to walk and talk as early as possible. But all too soon, we find ourselves saying things like "No, don't go there!" or "Don't say that. That's not nice." How about this one? "Where did you hear that? You are not allowed to say that!" It's easy to let encouragement fade as impatient instruction takes over when our children grow. Therefore, encouragement actually might feel like work, and it has to become a discipline. It helps to be proactive when it comes to encouraging your precious princess, a process that stems from being continually encouraged yourself.

As you spend time being encouraged, it will naturally overflow. So intentionally set up gentle reminders to share words of affirmation. Post a note inside the kitchen cupboard that says, "Remember to say, 'I love you.'" Or leave a note for yourself in her playroom that says, "You were a good girl just now," to remind you to affirm her. Or place the list of the fruit of the Spirit someplace to help you reflect on the fruit apparent in your daughter's heart today so that you can encourage her by sharing how you're seeing it in her life.

Our prayer is that you will embrace words of encouragement that come your way instead of replying, "Oh, don't say that. That really isn't me." Other people often see things in us that we haven't embraced or realized. But we tend to be our own harshest critics, and our daughters might follow in our footsteps by disbelieving our words of encouragement to them. Therefore, remember you are her example! Embrace encouragement as well as imparting it, so it will become a twofold blessing. You will both be filled with more joy and contentment as the fruit of kindness blooms in both of your hearts.

Princess of Kindness

It's heartwarming to see a girl treat friends, younger children, and the elderly with kindness. Praise your daughter every time you catch her being kind.

I (Karen) found a great example in my seven-year-old granddaughter, Elizabeth, who demonstrated kindness while tapping in to her passion for art.

Elizabeth: The Art Train

Elizabeth's mom, Darlene, homeschools her five children. She has a special room for crafts next to their home classroom and encourages her children to spend free time being creative with crafts and experiments. She also curtained off an area for a reading nook so the children could have quiet time and a spot to rest or relax.

One day Elizabeth noticed her mom looked tired. She asked, "Mom, do you need a little rest?"

Her mom, suffering from a major migraine, nodded.

Elizabeth said, "I'll fix things in a little while." Darlene wondered what her daughter had in mind.

Elizabeth went to the schoolroom and set up some crafts. She pulled out paints and paper, thought of quiet games, and put the supplies needed on another table. Then she went downstairs and told her mom to take a rest.

"Toot, toot!" Elizabeth called as she chugged around. Her younger brother Thomas yelled, "A train! I want to be on your train."

"Come aboard!" she said.

Her sisters and older brother also joined the train. Then they all headed upstairs and spent the next ninety minutes playing quietly. They painted pictures, and Elizabeth helped them make frames from colored paper. She taught them to make paper flowers to decorate the room.

After a nice nap, Darlene walked in and said, "Wow. It looks like you all had fun."

Everyone giggled and showed their mom what they made. Darlene gave Elizabeth a big hug and said, "Thank you so much for being kind and watching everyone. I had such a good rest."

Elizabeth continues to take her siblings on the "Craft Train" when she hears her mom say, "I need some quiet time to read my Bible," or "I need a nap." Her mom sometimes hears Elizabeth whisper, "Come on, Mommy needs us to be quiet. Let's go on the choo-choo train."

Elizabeth looks through craft supplies, the big craft jar, and craft books for ideas for future quiet times. She asks her mom to help her gather supplies if she needs anything special.

They've made jewelry and pom-pom pets and have used stamps and ink to make pictures. Sometimes Elizabeth asks them to name a design, and she draws them for her brothers and sisters to cut out and decorate. If someone is having a birthday, they make cards. For her grandpa's birthday, she had everyone make cutout cakes to go inside the cards. At other times she helped write promise cards for birthday gifts to come later. Elizabeth's gentle heart inspires her kindness.

Developing the Fruit of Kindness

Darlene is thankful her daughter is so kind. She reminds her children to think about the needs of others. She praises Elizabeth for letting her have some quiet time and using her creativity to help her siblings. Darlene works to develop the fruit of kindness in her daughter.

When Elizabeth had a bad day, her mother sat quietly and hugged her. Then she explained that her little girl needed to be calm and feel rested, suggesting she go to the book nook for a while. In a busy house with five children, Elizabeth found her spot to read, relax, and be refreshed. This experience helped her understand that we all need rest and quiet time.

It's important to help our children identify times when they feel blessed by someone's kindness. That will inspire them to perform compassionate and kind acts. When you notice that a smile, thoughtful word, sympathetic response, or generous act brings a smile to your daughter's face, take a moment to pause. Identify the act of kindness, and ask how it made her feel. Look for acts of kindness, especially those that change negative feelings into positive ones. Use these teachable moments to talk about compassion and kind responses. You'll be encouraging the growth of compassion that produces the fruit of kindness.

Pray with your daughter for opportunities to be kind to others. Rejoice when you see her act with kindness.

Fruitful Activities: Kindness

Fruit of the Spirit Verse

"Be kind and compassionate to one another, forgiving each other, just as in Christ God forgave you" (Ephesians 4:32, NIV).

The act of forgiveness keeps your little girl's heart soft. It helps her focus on God and what He wants her to do rather than thinking of herself.

Understand the Kindness Ripple Effect

Do a few experiments to show that one action can make a difference.

- Drop a rock into a pond, then watch the splash and the ripples it makes. The ripples get bigger as they expand outward. Explain that your daughter's kindness can cause another person to be kind—making a kindness ripple.

- Place celery in a glass of water. Add food coloring to the water and watch the celery gradually change color. Point out that kindness can change people, like something colorful added to their lives.

- Touch or pet a pom-pom or soft stuffed animal. Talk about how nice it feels. Then feel something hard, such as a rock. Talk about the difference. Ask if your child would want to be hugged by the rock or the stuffed animal. Chat about how kindness is like sending someone a soft hug, while being mean is like hitting her with a rock.

- Shine a light on a mirror, and watch how it reflects off the surface. See if you can take a second mirror to catch the light and pass it somewhere else. Explain how that's an illustration of the way kindness reflects love.

- Place an empty jar on a pie pan. Fill a bowl with water. Dip a thimble or tiny container in the water to fill the empty jar. Pour the water in the jar as you say something nice about the other person. Take turns and watch the jar fill up until it overflows. Talk about how kindness fills a heart until it overflows with kindness to give other people.

You're Kind When . . .

Talk about the following statements. Then, encourage your daughter to fill in the blanks by creating her own "you're kind when" ideas.

- You're kind when you listen to someone's problem and say you are sorry he or she feels sad.

- You're kind when you welcome people who visit and thank them when they leave.

- You're kind when you share your things.

- You're kind when you forgive people who hurt you, and pray for God to bless that person.

- You're kind when you're friendly. Be friendly with smiles and kind words and by inviting others to join you.

Treasure Box Addition

Talk about what the Bible says about kindness in Ephesians 4:32. Add a soft pom-pom to your treasure box as a reminder to be kind.

Appreciation Booklets

1. Take three sheets of paper and fold them in half to make a booklet of ten pages.

2. Decorate the cover, and write "10," "You're a Ten!" or "Ten Wonderful Things about You!"

3. On each page, write one thing you like about the person or one thing you've noticed about that person (great smile, is helpful, is kind, runs fast, sings well, etc.).

4. Give the booklet to the person and say, "I appreciate you!"

Sincere Compliments and Appreciation

Explain to your daughter that saying something nice that is true is a compliment. Here are some examples:

- I appreciate your smile.

- You have eyes that sparkle when you laugh.

- You always listen so attentively.

Appreciating people means letting them know you are grateful for them or their actions. Here are some examples. Can you think of others?

- Add to the thank-you: "Thanks for a great meal," or "Thanks for passing the carrots."

- Call a relative you don't see often to say hello.

- Tell a joke or sing a song to make Mom or Dad smile.

- Write and mail a letter to someone in the military.

- Draw a picture for a friend.

- Make up a cheer for your mom or other family member.

Random and Planned Acts of Kindness

Be kind to people, animals, and the earth with actions that show you care.

- Pick up litter.

- Make someone a snack.

- When you meet someone, learn his or her name.

- Learn something new about a friend, like a favorite color or game.

- Read to a younger child.

- Be a mother's helper to a neighbor.

- Shovel snow or rake a neighbor's driveway as a surprise.

- Leave flowers or a small treat at someone's door.

- Write the names of children in your class on slips of paper and place them in a jar. Each day draw a name, pray for the person, and try to do an act of kindness for him or her. It can be a simple smile or compliment.

- Clean out the car.

- Help with the laundry.

- Let a friend go first when playing a game.

- Pick up an item someone drops.

- Hold a door open.

Spotting Needs and Deeds of Kindness

Look around and see what's happening. Notice needs and
help if you can, or encourage the person in need. Observe
people in action who are helping or showing kindness.

- Notice if someone is alone.
- Notice if someone looks sad.
- Spot good deeds.
- Notice if your brother or sister helped you or cleaned up
  their room.
- Notice if a friend shared a toy.

Be Kind Campaign

Start a campaign to pass along kindness. Make heart-shaped
notes. Add kind words such as "God loves you." Write a note
on the back encouraging the one who receives it to pass the
kindness along. Place the notes in random spots, such as
books in your library (with permission) or car windshields.

Kindness Bookmarks

Have your mom type these words and print them out. Cut out
the rectangle of words and glue it on a long colored piece of
paper to make a bookmark. Punch a hole in the top and tie
on a yarn tassel.

K-eep helping others.
I-nclude others in your fun.
N-otice and compliment good deeds.
D-o good deeds.
N-urture a friendship to help it grow.
E-ncourage someone.
S-hare your things.
S-mile at everyone you meet.

Thoughtful Ideas

Here's a month of thoughtful actions! Read the thoughtful action in the morning and try to do it during the day. Fill in the dates starting with today.

Thoughtful Ideas	Date Completed
Compliment people today!	
Thank your mom after each meal.	
Clean your room to show you care about it.	
Call a friend and really listen.	
Smile at everyone today!	
Pray for your family.	
Politely invite a friend to church.	
Thank your pastor today for the sermon.	
Help set the table and clean up after meals.	
Pray for your teachers.	
Do something nice for a neighbor.	
Let others go first.	
Thank God for your family.	
Help clean up your home or yard.	
Greet people at church.	
Hug your mom and dad and say, "I love you."	
Pray for your friends.	
Make a snack for your family.	
Clean the bathroom you use.	
Make a thank-you card for a friend.	
Be cheerful all day.	
Help clean your Sunday school room.	
Feed birds and other creatures God made.	
Ask your mom what you can do to help her and do it!	

Thoughtful Ideas	Date Completed
Help a neighbor who has little children.	
Give old toys to the poor.	
If you hurt someone this week, say you are sorry.	
Do not complain today. Instead, smile.	

Dad and Daughter Activities

Showers of Blessings

Do something with your daughter to bless her mom. Here are some ideas:

- Make a meal or snack.
- Pick flowers or make a card together.
- Clean the table after a meal.

Do something with your daughter to be kind to another person. Add your own ideas to these:

- Wash a neighbor's car.
- Make sandwiches for the homeless.
- Call Grandma.
- Care for animals, real or stuffed.

Daddy's Encouraging Words

Consider the words you speak that fill your daughter's mind and heart. Make sure they are words that encourage her and not negative words.

Use words like these:

- Great effort.
- Thanks for helping.
- I love you.
- You are a princess.
- Good job!
- You made my day!

Mom's Tools

Kindness and Personality

Discover what motivates your daughter to be kind. Help her overcome weaknesses that breed selfishness or trigger mean responses. Individualize your responses based on her personality type.

A *Social Butterfly* naturally likes to be with others and cheer them up.

- Praise her when she reaches out to other people.
- Remind your daughter to give other people turns.
- Remind your little girl to invite loners into her circle of friends.
- Praise your daughter if she says something nice about a person who hurt her.

A *Born Leader* naturally wants to lead charity projects that reflect her kind heart.

- Make a kindness chart for your daughter to work on doing acts of kindness.

- Help your daughter list games her friends like to play, and encourage her to let the friend choose what to do at the next playdate.

- Encourage your daughter to express thanks more.

- Encourage your daughter to lead a charity drive, like collecting food for a pantry.

A *Princess of Order* is naturally thoughtful and kind.

- Encourage your child to write notes and draw pictures to say thanks.

- Think of a kind act to do together and then do it.

- Praise your daughter when she listens to her friends and empathizes with them.

Everyone's Friend is naturally diplomatic and kind except when giving in to sarcasm.

- Encourage your child to use humor kindly and not with sarcasm.

- Encourage her to praise others she sees being kind.

- Praise her for kindly helping friends settle a dispute.

- Praise your daughter for thinking of kind responses to people's comments or questions.

Dad's Toolbox

One of my favorite tools is the power screwdriver (something I learned from Chad). I keep one in my little toolbox. I like that I can change the head for any screw that's required for my household project. Those screws put things in place securely.

A father's encouragement is like that power screwdriver. Just as different screws fit different projects, your chosen words of affirmation will be highly valued and will secure your daughter's confidence in a way that no one else but Dad can. When she sleeps in her room for the first time by herself, and you share how proud you are that she's taken this big step to overcome her fears, she'll be so encouraged. A sweet good-night kiss seals your words. Your kind words expressing how pretty she looks are important to her, no matter how old she is. This reassurance is incredibly valuable coming from you. Remember, it is impossible to give sincere encouragement without kindness being present.

As you place the tool of encouragement into your toolbox, note that—just like the power screwdriver—it is one of the primary tools in your box. Encouragement is one of the most powerful gifts you can give your daughter.

I'll start being good when I turn 4.

ISABELLA, age 3, littlehoots.com

The Fruit of Patience and Self-Control

La Belle Jardinière proudly watches the fruit grow and ripen, but waits until the proper time to harvest it.

> Show-er Mothers
> Princess Attribute—Self-Control
> Fruit of the Spirit—Patience

SELF-CONTROL CAN BE ONE of the most challenging attributes for moms to demonstrate effectively. Why? Because of the repetition that is frequently required while parenting. Does this sound familiar? "How many times do I have to tell you not to let that back door slam shut?" It's the umpteenth time you made the request, and the door still slams!

A better alternative to repeating yourself? Take a few minutes to guide your daughter to change her ways by first showing her how to open and close the door without slamming it. This presents your child with a great example of self-control.

She will also see you exercising self-control when you hold your tongue and resist the impulse to lecture. Instead, help her understand why continually slamming the door shut might cause it to break. Or drive you to distraction. These calm moments enable you to feel better about yourself because you are demonstrating patience. Your little girl might be more willing to obey once she understands "why."

Victory's Story: Struggles with Anger

Victory says her children seem to be much like her in some ways, then completely the opposite in others. This truth reminds her to first learn about them as individuals instead of boxing them in with labels or assumptions. She easily identifies with two of her four children's relatively short fuses and their stubborn responses when they are emotionally hurt. She tells her story of dealing with anger in her own words:

It can be hard for me to accept an apology when I feel angry. I married a man who is quick to recognize his mistakes and ready to apologize. Sometimes his apologies come before I am even ready to forgive. I see this in my children too, and it often leads to chats about the fruit of self-control.

One afternoon, with the car full of kids, my third-born showed off her new reading skills. But she made an understandable mistake sounding out a word. Her big sisters giggled and corrected her. One glance in the rearview mirror and I saw her little arms folded across her chest, the steam pouring from her ears. I took the opportunity to remind her big sisters to encourage her new discoveries and give grace for her mistakes. They quickly apologized.

She refused their apologies and switched from victim to offender in a matter of seconds. She lashed out at her sisters with hurtful words. When the car was parked, I crawled to the backseat, hugged her, and talked to her about her errors. Her sisters had sincerely apologized, and she responded to their apology with angry words. I asked her to find some self-control, to let go of the anger, and to let the moment pass. We discussed how they all had made poor choices. But she was responsible for her reaction and now owed her sisters an apology. After a few tears, it blew over.

I instruct my children often to "take a deep breath" in order to give them the opportunity to recalibrate. Sometimes those few short seconds required to simply *breathe in* and *breathe out* can give us a brand-new perspective on things. I like to think of it as shutting my own mind down for just a few moments to let God take over. I can recall my mom doing the same—just simply breathing and letting that initial wave of emotion wash away.

We try to be real in our family. If I see one of my children acting out of impulse and emotion, I encourage that child to dig a little deeper to exercise self-control. We talk about how sometimes it is hard not to just act out how we feel. We discuss times when we have made matters worse by reacting and not filtering our negative responses to a person or situation. We need to pray and invite God into these moments, allowing His Spirit to work in us so that our responses honor Him, as well as others. Self-control means we don't do what we feel like doing, because we consider how our reaction will affect those around us, and because we recognize we need God's help to treat others well. How we treat others triggers consequences. When we acknowledge our lack of self-control, or other faults, we can better recognize ways we need the Lord's help.

Self-control is something I still struggle with as an adult at times, despite my years of relationship with Christ. Therefore, I need to give my kids grace as they grow and mature, knowing that He is the One who makes us good and right and holy.

How to Be a Mom Who Teaches by Showing

Modeling self-control is one of the best ways to teach it. When you observe your daughter yell about the same issue several times, and you respond calmly by discussing better ways to handle frustration, you are modeling and teaching self-control. At other times, you may teach her good habits by choosing healthy food to eat or faithfully exercising. Your perseverance, patience, and willpower will impress your children with your self-control.

Webster's Dictionary defines *self-control* as "restraint exercised over one's own impulses, emotions, or desires." Conviction immediately grips my heart as I (Doreen) reread this definition. As mothers, we are called to practice self-control and demonstrate patience. It's one of the greatest challenges as we live in such a fast-paced world.

As a young mom, my (Doreen's) patience began to dwindle after Brandy, our first little girl, began talking and walking. My second-born little girl, Kamy, had arrived prematurely with immature nerve endings. As a result, she cried and cried, which further undermined my self-control. I hoped time would help as her nerve endings developed. Meanwhile, my heart ached for her as *my* nerves grew raw from months of sleep deprivation.

I found myself grumpy, short-tempered, and wanting my husband, Chad, to get home as soon as possible from work each day. I would call him in the late afternoon asking, "How soon are you coming home?" I questioned whether or not he had to work overtime. Though we truly needed any overtime pay he could capture, at the time *my* needs seemed more important than our finances.

During those difficult days, I often snapped at Brandy unnecessarily. Then I'd dissolve into tears, asking her to forgive Mommy for speaking so harshly. At one point, I remember shaking my precious little infant because I was so frustrated with her crying. Then I wept uncontrollably. In that moment I realized I desperately needed help. I called my friend Emilie, asking her to please come immediately, because I had reached the end of my emotional rope and my self-control.

Fortunately, Emilie happened to be free and came immediately. By the time she arrived both girls were actually sleeping. What a godsend! I sobbed again with a tremendous amount of shame and guilt. Emilie wrapped her arms around me and let me cry for a few minutes. Then she assured me that God was not mad at me, which was my greatest fear.

Emilie sat me down and shared the importance of calling her, or someone else I might trust, before it was too late and I did something I deeply regretted. She said that asking for help—even if it was just calling and asking for prayer over the phone—could assist me in those moments. If no one was available, she encouraged me to take a deep breath and send up a quick prayer: "Help me, God!" She assured me that He answered even the shortest prayers. Truthfully, I had never considered either option because my pride or shame caused me to refrain from asking for help. Emilie's nonjudgmental words of comfort and encouragement set me on a new journey.

The next time I experienced excessive frustration because of Brandy's disobedience and Kamy's crying, I stopped and said, "Help me, God." I just stood there for a moment. Honestly, within seconds I felt the tightness in my chest loosen as a sense of calm came over me. I was able to speak to Brandy in an appropriate tone and gently picked up Kamy and took her to her room to cry it out. Things weren't perfect, but for the first time I saw evidence of self-control that demonstrated patience in me.

One day, after several weeks of calling Emilie, she encouraged me to find a verse about patience that I could post on my refrigerator as a reminder. I had been reading through the Psalms for the first time in my life and "happened upon a verse about patience." (I truly believe today these are God's timely words just for us.) "Be patient and you will finally win, for a soft tongue can break hard bones" (Proverbs 25:15, TLB).

Whoa! I couldn't believe what I read. I felt like I was winning as I saw the results of following Emilie's counsel. I realized that more gently correcting Brandy changed her disobedient spirit. My angry, frustrated voice created fear, but it had not changed her behavior. Kamy really wasn't crying less, but she began sleeping more. I felt grateful, because I could handle just about anything after some peaceful, uninterrupted hours of sleep.

Brandy was my quick learner, and it didn't take long before I saw the evidence of self-control in her that grew the fruit of patience. I often told her what a big girl she was because she set a good example for Kamy. Throughout the years, Kamy watched and learned from Brandy's life lessons. Therefore, Kamy required less discipline than Brandy ever did.

As Brandy entered high school, her growing self-control benefited her greatly as she applied this fruit to her academic studies. She eventually achieved excellent grades and honors. I especially noticed Brandy's fruit of patience when she became close friends with a physically disabled young woman who required much more assistance than most teens could manage. Yet for Brandy, the wealth of their friendship was worth any physical inconveniences. The fruit of patience in Brandy's life had resulted from learning self-control in her early years.

I hope sharing my story helps you today to see that you are not alone. I am praying for you already, that you, too, will recognize the fruit of patience growing in your life as you become more self-controlled. Taking control over your emotions enables you to face your challenges with a greater measure of patience. Your example will inspire your daughter to learn self-control.

Princess of Patience

Children live in an age of immediate gratification. Microwaves, fast food, and search engines on computers make waiting seem unnecessary. That makes it harder to foster patience in girls and to teach them to be considerate and controlled when they need to wait. In the following story, we can see how Amy worked hard with her daughter to bring about needed changes in self-control and patience.

How Bella Grew in Self-Control

At home Amy relaxed as she saw her children were having a nice time together. Suddenly, Bella's scream pierced the air, and soon she added kicking and throwing objects to her screams.

Bella's tantrum continued; Amy didn't even know what triggered it. She felt helpless to stop her daughter or prevent her many outbursts. Amy had learned to move Bella to a safe spot or to move objects out of harm's way. Her daughter could go from joyful excitement to a rage in seconds, like a tornado tearing through the house. It seemed that any emotion could overwhelm her and trigger a full-blown tantrum. Amy spoke quietly and reminded Bella she loved her and that God loved her. After calming down, Bella cried and seemed embarrassed, even scared of her own uncontrollable emotions.

Bella said, "Mom, I need to eat more of the fruit of self-control."

Amy and Bella set out to work on self-control and those raging emotions. Thankfully, she didn't go into a rage outside her home. Amy tried to track the little girl's rages, identifying causes as well as what helped calm her down. They prayed daily for the fruit of the Spirit, especially self-control and patience.

Her mom, dad, or grandmother started asking Bella, "Are you hungry for some fruit?" as a signal that she should check her emotions and pray. This helped Bella stop and think about how she felt. It gave her time to take deep breaths and relax instead of getting wound up. Her mom discovered Bella had food allergies that triggered unrest. She also started to do physical stretches and drawing in order to unwind and regain self-control.

Bella remembers the days she lacked self-control and empathizes with a boy in her Sunday school class. The friend is a few years older and autistic. When she or the class helper notices his emotional temperature rising, they quietly leave the room and walk with him to a quiet place. Bella patiently reminds him that she has also had tantrums. She prays with him, "God, thank You for Your fruits. We need more of them, especially self-control." They accept and understand him, and he calms more easily with just the two of them beside him. He uses a stress toy, and Bella is teaching him to sketch as an outlet for his emotions.

Developing the Fruit of Patience

It's wonderful to see your princess overcome a difficulty, then turn to patiently help someone else with a similar problem. It's a time to rejoice in her budding patience.

Patience is the ability to bear trials without grumbling;

quiet, steady perseverance; or even-tempered care. That's quite a high standard. Small wonder that it's hard to maintain patience for long periods or when things go wrong. It's easy to snap and release the built-up anger or inner complaints when we feel hurt or slighted. It's difficult to remain calm when we are frustrated while learning a new skill. It's hard to wait. Patience is a fruit that's hard to grow and reminds us of how a farmer must wait for fruit to grow through a long season that also takes continual nurturing.

The first step in cultivating patience is to stop rushing and slow down. Take time with your daughter in play and work, including dressing and fixing hair. When teaching a new skill, do it for a little while before frustration starts. Explain that you'll work on it more the next day. Her little mind needs time to process the skill.

Cultivate patience by developing a sense of time and cultivating ideas to fill periods of waiting. Use a stopwatch or minute hourglass to show how much can be done in one minute and yet how quickly it passes. You can time getting dressed, setting the table, and singing a song. Check how many jumps a child can take or how far she can run in sixty seconds. Create a waiting bag to use for delays or expected times of waiting, such as in a doctor's office. Include books, finger puppets, paper and crayons, and quiet games. Discuss how those are also times to use her imagination and think of things to do when she is back home or with a friend.

Encourage your daughter to share her skills to patiently teach a younger sibling or friend. Praise your daughter's patience, especially when she is taking time to slowly help another person or to complete a tedious task well.

Work on strategies that release frustration and bottled emotions in a healthful way, such as counting fingers, taking deep breaths, praying for people involved in the delay, and thinking happy thoughts.

Time is a gift, and wisely using extra minutes of waiting is a blessing. Patience is a fruit to be valued.

Fruitful Activities

A princess must develop self-control to continue to produce patience.

In an instant world, patience is difficult to cultivate. Gaining control of her emotions is the first step in learning to wait. Learning how to use the moments of waiting helps a girl become more patient.

Fruit of the Spirit Verse

"Let us not grow weary of doing good, for in due season we will reap, if we do not give up" (Galatians 6:9, ESV).

As mothers, we understand weariness and lack of sleep. We must continue our parenting work if we want to raise a real princess of the kingdom. It will be worth the effort.

Wait-a-Minute Fun and Other Activities to Teach Patience

Use timed activities to help your child learn how to tell time, wait with grace, and fill the minutes with simple activities.

- Set a timer for five, ten, or fifteen minutes. Let that signal you'll be ready to help your daughter or to transition to a different activity, such as going to bed.

- Time your daughter for one minute in jumping, skipping, cleaning up, reciting ABCs, counting, saying memory verses, etc.

- Ask your daughter to close her eyes and hold up her hand when she thinks a minute has ended.

- Note the time at meals, bedtime, nap time, or other routine activity to help your child develop her sense of time.

- Fill minutes of waiting with making funny faces, telling jokes, or telling silly stories.

- Limit how quickly you respond to every request. Let your child wait until you complete a task.

- Use play to teach patience. Play games that require taking turns, and do puzzles.

- Bake yeast bread and cookies. Chat about how dough needs time to rise and cookies need time to bake.

- Get a treat now or wait one minute and get two (besides sweets you can use pretzels or carrots— something healthy).

- String cereal necklaces to practice patience, and make other time-consuming crafts.

Self-Control Helps

Make a chart with rules and consequences. Include positive consequences for following rules. Use pictures instead of writing for younger girls. Be sure to look at the chart and remind your child about any broken rule. State it simply in short sentences, such as: "It's not okay to hit your sister. I see you feel angry, but you need to respect your sister. Use words to say you are angry."

My Patience Bag

Fill a bag or backpack with quiet activities for a child to use when she must wait. Here are some ideas:

- books
- crayon, pencils, and paper
- chenille stems
- finger puppets
- small doll and clothes
- pocket-sized games, especially magnetic ones when your child is old enough for small pieces
- small felt board and felt pieces
- A coin to play "Here's the Coin": One person hides her hands behind her back and puts the coin in one hand. She makes fists of both hands and brings them to the front. The other person needs to guess which hand holds the coin. If the person guesses correctly, she gets to hide the coin.

Rule	Consequence for disobeying	Consequence for obeying
Clean rooms before dessert	No cleaning, no dessert	Dessert, and if done for a week, extra time for a story
No hitting, pushing, or hurting someone physically	Person can use one of your toys for thirty minutes	Fun hands-on activity like a puzzle or board game
No using mouth to hurt someone (no hurtful words or biting)	If you bite someone, everyone else gets a snack party (you already ate a sweet snack by biting a sweet person)	Big smiles and a breath mint

Rule	Consequence for disobeying	Consequence for obeying
Speak softly without yelling or screaming	Time-out followed by a whispered chat	Praise for controlling tongue
Pass nicely and don't throw toys or objects	Pick up thrown objects, and one of your favorite objects will be put up for a few days	Do this for a week, and you get a tea party with Mom
Do chores before playing	Toys will be taken away, and you will need to go back and finish the job	Hooray! You get to play!
Obey your parent without unkind words	Miss a sweet snack, and still need to obey the original instruction or request	Praise for a good job and star on your chart or marble in the jar

Seed Sprouting

Sprout seeds in a jar. Chat about how the seeds grew as everyone slept and played. They continue to grow. We can't make it happen faster.

Dad and Daughter Activities

Count Your Blessings Together

Make a statement, and encourage your daughter to repeat it or add her own. Here are some ideas:

- God blessed me with you.

- God blessed me with a great day.

- God blessed me with an imagination.

- God blessed me with my family.

- God blessed me with a friend who _____.

Bicycle Lessons

Teach your daughter to ride a bicycle when she is old enough. Explain why she must slow down to take a curve and maintain control of the bike. Set up an obstacle course once she is a proficient rider. Then chat about obstacles in life, including things that make her angry. Talk about ways to maintain control and steer clear of problems.

Mom's Tools

Emotional Coaching

Be an emotion coach to cultivate your child's emotional responses.

- Avoid the tendency to think or say, "Get over it," a phrase that dismisses feelings.

- Avoid the disapproving style that tells a child she shouldn't feel a certain way or that anger and other negative feelings are a sign of weakness.

- Avoid the "let it be" approach that accepts all emotional responses, even rages and tantrums.

- Coach by empathizing and guiding, so that your daughter understands how emotions work, how to manage them, and how to get along with others.

- Observe and note your child's emotions.

- Connect and talk about your child's emotions and responses to them.

- Listen to your child, including how she expresses feelings.

- Name the emotions to help your child identify her feelings.

- Seek solutions together. Brainstorm ideas.

- Read books and stories where children deal with emotions.

- Talk about emotions after your daughter is calm.

- Discuss solutions she tried and what happened.

- Put the emotions felt in perspective by discussing excitement after a party or anger after a tantrum.

- Pray together for the fruits of peace, gentleness, and self-control.

Marble System

Each time your daughter does something to display a fruit of the Spirit, let her put a marble in her fruit of the Spirit jar. Examples:

- Waiting to talk until Mommy hangs up the phone.

- Letting a sibling go first in a game.

- Doing a chore with a smile.

When she "earns" fifty marbles, she gets a date with one of her parents, and her choice of where and with whom. This could be playtime at a park, a visit to a museum, or a meal at a restaurant.

Don't be "jarred" if the marbles don't seem to increase. It may be a sign that you are not encouraging your daughter or even noticing her actions.

Make Self-Control Rewarding

Teach your daughter to come when called. Promote this response by calling her at times to give a reward, a hug, or praise. Give points, stickers, or marbles to add to a jar when she shows self-control.

Cut the Whining

It's hard to listen to anyone complain and whine, especially if they go on and on. The first complaint is probably a call for empathy and help. Continued whining reflects dissatisfaction and the need for attention.

Cut out continuous whining by addressing problems early and actively listening to your daughter.

1. Show empathy. If shoes are too tight, express sympathy for her feet hurting, suggest changing them, and talk about setting a date to shop for new shoes.

2. Reduce whining by helping your child learn to express needs in a positive way and tone. Reflect the need with an example of a polite sentence.

3. Observe triggers that cause your little girl to whine. This may be tiredness, hunger, or boredom. Help her realize she is tired and needs to take a quiet break, or that she needs a snack if hungry. Help your daughter with a posted list of what to do when she is bored. This could be communicated with pictures or words, depending on her age.

4. Don't reinforce whining by giving in, but do be empathetic.

5. Use some simple songs that include verses or Scriptures as reminders not to grumble, such as "Do everything without finding fault or arguing" (Philippians 2:14).

"Welcome others into your homes without complaining" (1 Peter 4:9).

"Let the words you speak always be full of grace. . . . Then you will know how to answer everyone" (Colossians 4:6).

"Don't let any evil talk come out of your mouths. Say only what will help to build others up and meet their needs. Then what you say will help those who listen" (Ephesians 4:29).

6. Turn it into a time of gratitude. So, if your child is hungry, remind her to thank God that there is plenty of food and a meal will be ready soon.

Patience, Self-Control, and Personality

Discover the motivations in your daughter that help her be patient and self-controlled. Help her overcome weaknesses that breed stubbornness, impatience, and lack of control.

A *Social Butterfly* wants attention but loves social time.

- Reward patience with time for friends via phone or in person.
- Help your child restate a whine into a polite request.
- Have a patience bag ready to go for trips.

A *Born Leader* is goal-and-time oriented, less patient with waiting.

- List ideas of things to do while waiting, such as reading a book or creating a plan for a project.
- Encourage your daughter to teach a skill to a friend or younger child.
- Help your child learn healthy ways to vent anger.

A *Princess of Order* fears being noticed and wants to know the routine or plan.

- Discuss upcoming plans with your daughter so she will be willing to wait.
- Encourage her to draw or write about frustrations.
- Help your child cheer other people who win a game and work at improving their skills rather than comparing abilities.

Everyone's Friend is relaxed, not worried about time, but tends to procrastinate.

- Encourage your child to respond when asked and to be on time to avoid trying the patience of others.
- Praise her for being a peacemaker and calming others who show anger.
- Use praise to encourage your daughter to keep working at a new skill.

Dad's Toolbox

I remember how many different-sized clamps hung on the wall of my father's workshop. Yet the clamps had no value at all if glue wasn't present. When my father placed glue on two pieces of wood, then clamped them together, he would say, "Okay, now we must wait." He'd clean up his shop and head into the house for dinner. For me, the waiting was the hardest part, because I wanted to see the whole piece put together, right away.

Isn't self-control just like a clamp? It is the force that holds your raging emotions together at times. It clamps your mouth shut when everything in you wants to explode in anger, because maybe your little girl just won't stop whining.

Dad, modeling self-control truly reveals one of the strongest disciplines in life and confirms a highly coveted godly trait: patience. Your self-control will demonstrate to your daughter that she can control her own behavior. Simple demonstrations of patience with your daughter might include something like listening to her favorite song over and over. Or responding positively when she brings you her favorite book—the one you've read countless times—saying, "Daddy! Let's read it again." When you do, that is patience.

Remember that as you pull out and use your patience tool, it will reveal your self-control!

While we try to teach our children all about life, our children teach us what life is all about.

ANGELA SCHWINDT, homeschooling mom

The Fruit of Love in Your Princess's Life

La Belle Jardinière is a servant who brings out the best in seeds sown, then shares her produce with others.

Servant Mothers
Princess Attribute—Server
Fruit of the Spirit—Love

MOST MOTHERS, by nature, have a servant's heart when it comes to taking care of their children. The call to serve our husbands, however, can be more challenging. Yet how important it is for a child to experience the love between his or her mother and father. Our heavenly Father's love is fully demonstrated in the way parents love and serve each other.

This kind of servant love can be seen in simple acts of service. Mom makes Dad his favorite snack and gives it to him while he watches the football game, for instance. Or Dad brings Mom her slippers when she sits down to rest after dinner. Simple acts of love such as these turn hearts toward each other.

It's so precious to see the result of this modeling when

your daughter, without being asked, makes her daddy his favorite snack or brings you your slippers! She quickly learns that serving delights the hearts of others and is a true act of love.

I understand that, like me (Doreen), you may never have felt that fatherly love in your childhood years. My parents loved each other, but I hungered to experience the parental love I felt was missing as a child. Thankfully, God used my grandmother (my father's mother) to fill some of that void. I hope someone filled that void in your life, too.

Doreen's Story: A Grandmother's Servant Love

I (Doreen) had spent the night at my grandmother's home. I remember awakening out of a twilight sleep early that morning to the sound of her voice. She was singing, quietly talking, and then gently weeping.

As a six-year-old, I was curious. Her bedroom door was open a crack, so I tiptoed up to it and peeked in. She wore a long nightgown that must have been made of white linen; it gently hugged her frame, and simple ruffles graced its sleeves. Her graying hair flowed down to the middle of her back, and her hands were folded, her head humbly bowed. She looked like an angel as she knelt, praying, beside her bed.

Her sweet presence was such a contrast to her usual practical appearance. Many times I'd enter her home to greet her standing by her old gas stove making fresh tortillas—always the crowning glory of every meal she made. She wore her hair pulled straight back in a bun, and she never wore makeup. She dressed in homemade dresses with no frills, and she wore no jewelry. Her nylon stockings were always rolled down to her ankles above her loafers.

I seldom focused long on her appearance, because the moment she set eyes on me she would exclaim, "Miya! How are you? You look beautiful today. Tell me about school. Tell me about church!" She would hand me a fresh tortilla hot from the griddle, a tortilla shaped like Mickey Mouse, or a bunny, or other fun shape. Then she'd say, "Sit down and tell me everything, my girl. I want to know all about you!" Week after week, year after year, she richly validated me as someone she treasured deeply. I always felt confident of her love.

As I peeked into the bedroom door that morning, she noticed my presence and called my name, waving for me to join her. I knelt next to her, and she drew me close with one arm and continued to pray. She prayed God's blessing upon my father, my aunt, and my uncles. She sweetly sang songs of worship, then prayed for me. I felt the warmth of her love for God, others, and me through her prayer that day. When she finished, she stood and said, "I must get dressed, and you must get ready to go. Your mother and father will be here soon."

Minutes later her bedroom door opened. I looked at her and took note immediately of her shoes. She wore high heels! I scanned her from her shoes on up. Her nylons were rolled up past her knees. She wore a lovely, navy blue dress with a beautiful white embroidered collar. A fox-fur stole around her shoulders cuddled her neck. She had applied a light shade of lipstick that perfectly shaped her lips. Her pillbox hat sat securely on her head, its simple veil draped over her forehead. Her posture was straight as an arrow, and her matching purse graced the arm that carried her Bible.

"Grandma," I exclaimed, "you are so pretty. No, Grandma, you are not just pretty, you are beautiful! Where are you going dressed like that?"

"Miya, I am going to meet the King! I am a daughter of the King," she proclaimed boldly. A chill ran down my back as I immediately sat up a little straighter. Her confident stance and words made me feel as if I were in the presence of royalty.

Suddenly the doorbell rang, signaling the arrival of my mom and dad. They quickly ushered me into the car, and we left for church. As she waited for her ride, my grandmother threw kisses and called out, "I love you," until I was out of sight.

I forgot that moment until forty years later. In the spring of 1999, I was asked, "Do you have a frame of reference that would enable you to speak on the topic of 'A Daughter of the King'?"

Immediately God brought back the memory of my grandmother preparing for church, as clearly as if it had been yesterday. "Yes, I do, and I believe I can," I stated with God-given confidence. Weeks later I shared my grandmother's story and felt it was the highlight of my presentation.

How to Be a Servant Mom

Today, as I remember my grandmother, I recall her incredible confidence that she knew "whose" she was! She embraced the love of her heavenly Father and did not hesitate to boldly ask His best for everyone she loved as she prayed. She had a servant heart.

As I grew up, I watched my grandmother closely. She was a seamstress and a pastor's wife, and she was always serving others. I never saw her serve others without her service being seasoned with joy and humility. I don't remember a time that she wasn't prepared to help others with her gifts. She frequently sent meals to poor families in the church or neighborhood when she learned of their needs. As a seamstress, she helped young women who couldn't afford to buy their wedding gowns by creating them for little cost. She sewed or crocheted tea towels or doilies, bringing them as gifts when invited for a meal. She integrated every act of service with words of love and encouragement for those she encountered. She forgave others for hurtful deeds or words. She carried her pain and life's struggles with grace and forgiveness. That included forgiving my grandfather for leaving the ministry and divorcing her after thirty years of marriage. Yet the evidence of love continued to be beautifully displayed throughout her life, as she served others in word and deed.

What a role model my grandmother was for me as well as others throughout her lifetime! As a little girl, I prayed that I might grow up and be just like her.

My mother also heaped blessings on me. She demonstrated her love by serving our family well. She took wonderful care of my sister and me. There was always a good meal on the table. Our home and clothes were clean. Our father provided a safe home and security for us. As little girls, all our basic needs were met. However our parents rarely ever said the words "I love you." They echoed their own parents' approach to child rearing, an approach that didn't include intentional words of loving affirmation.

Generational parenting is a natural process and will always continue to be. As a new parent in the 1970s, I wanted to follow my mother's footsteps in the way she cared for us. But I also wanted to be like my grandmother, making sure to speak words of love on a regular basis to my girls, knowing how much I'd missed hearing verbal expressions of love at home.

Chad and I invested in intentional speech when our girls were young, and it bore good fruit. Today, greetings or goodbyes between my girls still include hugs and the words "I love you." This has turned into a legacy. I delight in imparting words of value into my grandchildren's lives, cheering on their godly character and sharing my pride in their achievements—just as my grandmother did for me. An ultimate moment today is when my grandchildren initiate those words of love before I do!

Acts of service are a big part of my daughters' and grandchildren's lives now. They bake Christmas cookies and give them to the neighbors during the holidays. They helped a mom with a debilitating illness and her six children by making meals and doing housecleaning. Wonderful opportunities like these enable our daughters to see and experience the value of servant love.

Remember, your words of love serve your daughter's soul, just as your deeds meet her needs.

Princess of Love

Servant love is all about putting others first and reaching out to show love. It's not natural, but it can be learned and reinforced through experience, examples, and praise. For instance, see how Rebecca demonstrated servant love through flowers she grew herself.

Rebecca's Seeds of Love

Rebecca gently dropped marigold seeds into egg carton sections she had filled with soil. Each day she used an eyedropper and watered them. Soon the seeds sprouted. After a few weeks, she replanted each one into a plastic cup. She enjoyed this early spring activity as we waited for the days to warm up.

Finally, spring came and I (Karen) suggested that we plant the flowers outside. Rebecca said she had other plans. She borrowed a wagon from a neighbor and filled it with the blossoming, leafy plants. Then she pulled the wagon to each front door in our little housing area, knocked, and gave the plants to neighbors. She said, "God loves you and gave us these pretty flowers. I want you to have one that I grew." The neighbors smiled and thanked her. Many planted them in their window boxes or garden areas.

I beamed with joy as I saw my young girl choose to serve others and give them the fruit of her labor as she shared her faith. As she grew up, she continued to give handmade gifts to friends and family. When she had a job delivering newspapers, she made Christmas ornaments for all her customers.

Rebecca is grown now, and she still loves to make gifts to give others. She cooks gourmet treats, mixes fancy olive oils, and creates special scrapbook albums as gifts. She creates cards for the gifts and writes messages reflecting God's love. Her heart is open to expressing love through service.

Developing the Fruit of Servant Love

Understanding love and following Christ's example as a servant helps us nurture servant hearts in our daughters. True love is from God, and His ultimate gift is His Son, Jesus Christ. The biblical meaning of *love* is "a purposeful commitment to sacrificial action for another." It puts the other person first (see Luke 10:27). Service means meeting the needs of others.

God wants us to love others. He gave us a command to love others as He loved us (see John 15:12). Jesus showed His love by serving others, meeting needs, and ultimately dying that we might be saved.

That's counter to our human nature. Though we loved our little girl from the very start, we quickly realized that as a little baby, she considered herself the center of the universe. Babies cry to have their own needs met. As children grow, it takes parental diligence to help each one develop an attitude of service, looking outward instead of inward.

Our first step is to show our love by serving our families and others. It can be hard to do laundry or prepare a snack when you're weary, but those actions show love. My daughter first helped me make and give neighbors Christmas breads, a tradition I still enjoy. She also helped make brownies or bread for new neighbors who moved in and meals for sick neighbors. As a family, we made sandwiches for the homeless and added paper hearts that said, "Jesus loves you." Serving others flows more naturally when it is part of a family's focus.

Noticing the service of others helps make service a priority. When neighbors gave us meals after the birth of another child or when I had pneumonia, I expressed my thanks and praised the loving acts to my children. I tried to remember to thank clerks at stores when they made an extra effort to help us. When you express thanks for acts of service (whether it's someone opening a door, picking up a dropped item, or praying for you), you highlight the way loving service brings joy to hearts.

Pray with your daughter each morning and ask God how you can each bless someone else. That helps you focus on loving and serving others.

Fruitful Activities

Christian love is not the same as our culture's typical use of the word *love*. Christian love is sacrificial and requires a commitment to care for the needs of others.

Fruit of the Spirit Verse

"Here is my command. Love each other, just as I have loved you" (John 15:12).

Fill your daughter's heart with love, so she experiences unconditional love from you and from God. Be a role model by loving others through your actions and words.

Treasure Box Addition

Cut a little heart from fabric or paper and add it to the box. Read the story of Jesus inviting the children to come to Him in Luke 18:15-17. Talk about how much Jesus loves them. Read about Dorcas in Acts 9:36-43, and discuss the way Dorcas showed her love by helping others. Explain that her friends were sad when Dorcas died, so they asked Peter to help. He prayed, and God brought her back to life. Ask questions and discuss how the story shows ways people love one another.

Be a Loving Friend

Everyone enjoys friends. Explain to your daughter that it's important to be a good friend and to show love to our friends. Share the following ideas to help her with actions that demonstrate love.

- Greet your friend with a smile and warm hello.

- Ask your friend how she is doing, and really listen to her answer.

- Share and take turns when you play together.

- When a friend hurts or upsets you, take a deep breath and remain calm. Explain in words what happened and what she did that hurt. For example, "You pulled the toy I was using out of my hands. That hurt my hands, and I was enjoying the toy. I feel sad."

- Forgive your friend for hurting you.

- Always say nice things about your friend to others.

- Ask your friend what she likes to play and do, and plan times for her favorite activities.

- Let your friend know what you enjoy doing.

- Thank your friend for playing with you.

Friendship Crafts

Make something for your friend to show her that you care.

- *"You're Great" Place Mat.* Use a large sheet of card stock. Decorate it with pictures cut from magazines, stickers, and words that express great qualities about your friend. Add a photo of the two of you together. Cover it with clear plastic adhesive or slide it into a large Ziploc bag.

- *Friendship Jewelry.* Use colored beads of pasta to string together a necklace or bracelet. The colors can express love and friendship:

  - Red is for love.

  - Blue stands for always being friends, no matter where under the sky you might be.

  - Green is for growing friendship.

  - Yellow symbolizes sunny times to share laughter.

  - Orange is for "Orange you glad we're friends?"

  - Purple, a color of royalty, stands for being a princess friend.

  - White is for forgiveness.

  - Black stands for your promise to pray for your friend when she's sad.

  - Brown is for parties with chocolate, tea, and togetherness.

- *Framed with Love.* Take photos of you with your friend. Print them out. Frame them with a store-bought frame or one made from tongue depressors or colored paper and cardboard. Decorate the frame with hearts.

- *Crowned with Love.* Make your princess friend a crown. Add words or stickers that state her good qualities or fruit of the Spirit you see in her.

Generous Deeds of Service

Encourage your princess to serve others with some of these choices:

- Pass out the plants you grew in chapter 4.
- Draw pictures for friends and neighbors.
- Open doors for your mom.
- Help serve meals.
- Help clean up after meals.
- Play with a younger child.
- When a friend comes to play, serve her a snack.
- Give away toys and clothes you don't need anymore.
- Buy extra school supplies for needy children.
- As a family, make sandwiches for the homeless.
- Make a centerpiece for the table.
- Make name tags for friends coming to dinner.

Handy Helper Booklet

Trace your child's hand on a folded piece of paper with her little finger lying beside the fold. Cut it out, but don't cut the fold.

Let your child write ways to serve others on each finger. Younger children can draw or dictate words. They can pray for family and friends, help around the house, give away toys and clothes, pick up litter, and so forth. Keep the booklet in view so your child can look through it each day to choose ways to serve others.

Learning to Give Up

Give up time or things to help others. That's *sacrifice* and shows true love. Invite your daughter to:

- Give up dessert or snacks to save the money to help others.
- Give up some of your school supplies for needy children.

- Give away favorite books or toys to help a needy child.

- Give time to pick up litter at church or a park.

- Give time to do extra chores to let Mom have a break. Fold laundry, set the table, take out garbage, wash walls, or do other chores you don't normally do.

Dad and Daughter Activities

Serve Together

Find a way you and your daughter can serve together at church, such as picking up litter with you once a month.

Be a Servant

Let your daughter see your servant attitude as you perform little acts for others, such as holding a door open.

Serve her. Do little things for her, like fix her hair, help her put on her coat, or buckle her up.

Praise Her Servant Heart

Let your princess serve you. Let her do little things for you, such as fix a snack or hold a tool while you make repairs.

Ask for her help. Show your appreciation with a smile, hug, and word of thanks.

Mom's Tools

Sacrificial Love Offerings

Jesus gave His life for us as a sacrifice. Talk about the meaning of the word *sacrifice* with your daughter. Let her put the money saved in a little bank or purse to collect and hand in weekly or monthly at church. Let her also do extra chores to earn quarters to give to those in need.

Chat about following Jesus, the true Servant King. Share these important ABCs:

Admit that you disobey and sin and that you need Jesus.
Believe Jesus died to save you.
Call on Jesus to make you His child, a princess of His
  kingdom.

Family Projects of Service

One of the best ways to nurture a servant heart is through serving others as a family. Whether you help an elderly neighbor with yard work, collect clothes for a shelter, or serve one another in little deeds at home, do it together.

Choose activities where your daughter can really help and not just watch. Let your child help plan and choose what to do.

If a new neighbor moves in, use the opportunity to talk about showing love to the new family. Provide ideas such as baking a special treat, watching the younger children so parents can unpack, or digging up a plant to give.

If you want to serve at church, look for opportunities to serve as a family, such as helping to collect toys at Christmas or helping with the church grounds.

Take photos of your daughter serving others, and make a little booklet of those pictures. Or post a few of the photos on the refrigerator as reminders that she blesses others and shows love through her actions.

Coaching Your Princess in Forgiving Others

Forgiveness can be hard on your little girl. She may still feel angry and want to hold a grudge. To illustrate the power of forgiveness, start by rubbing a little dirt on your daughter's hand. Have her take a sniff. It might be smelly. Ask if she'd like that dirt to remain there forever. It's not fun to have a dirty hand, and it's not healthy. Talk about germs that may hide in the dirt.

Then wash off the dirt. Talk about how clean her hand looks. Take a sniff and see if it smells nice too. Chat about how anger is like dirt that gets in your heart, and forgiveness washes it away, leaving your heart clean and sweet smelling inside. Forgiving someone who hurts us is part of what it means to follow Jesus and love like He did.

Christian Love and Personality

Foster your daughter's servant attitude and Christian love according to her personality.

A *Social Butterfly* likes social activities.

- Encourage your daughter to show love to friends and to serve them.
- Let your daughter invite friends for a party or playtime and plan snacks and activities.
- Make and deliver tray decorations to a nursing home.

A *Born Leader* wants a plan and likes to take charge.

- Collect canned goods from your neighbors for a food pantry.
- Work together to organize the garage or some other messy area of your home.
- Make simple games to give friends or organize a game day for friends.

A *Princess of Order* likes a sense of direction and quiet activities, and prefers to follow.

- Write a letter to a person serving overseas in the military.
- Color pictures for friends and family or community workers.
- Push stray carts in the parking lot to designated areas.

Everyone's Friend likes humor, peace, and being beloved.

- Tell jokes and stories to a sick or lonely relative via the Internet.
- Encourage your daughter to befriend someone who is not popular.
- Help make bread or muffins for a neighbor.

Dad's Toolbox

Love is the glue that holds it all together. It's like a beautiful wooden bowl that has been glued, shaped, sanded, and stained to serve a delicious dish to share with others. Love is what motivates us to serve.

In the early 1950s, my paternal grandfather often fed the poor in Los Angeles on the streets of Skid Row. He had a love for his Hispanic culture and struggling families. My husband, Chad, and my father enjoyed traveling together to an orphanage in Mexico, bringing their tools for many needed repairs.

Just as my husband and father united with others to build and repair, the tool of love unites hearts. As your daughter begins to enjoy some of the same things you do, together you will become like-minded, which can lead to opportunities to serve together. Serving comes in so many different forms. Whatever it might look like in your family, your love will grow in serving together.

When you use your tool of service, may your daughter see the love in your heart that embraces her as well as others.

You can learn many things from children. How much patience you have, for instance.

FRANKLIN P. JONES, American humorist

10

Continuing the Journey as a Daughter of the King

A silver basket or cornucopia heaped with fruit
demonstrates the hard labor of La Belle Jardinière,
who blesses others with a healthful bounty.

> Joyous Mothers
> Fruitful Princesses
> Blessed Daughters

PARENTS DELIGHT IN seeing their children develop positive character qualities, evidence of the fruit of the Spirit growing in their lives. It's also a joy to reward or celebrate successful character growth in our children.

Upon completion of this journey, it's time to celebrate the fruit of the Spirit you have seen growing in the heart of your princess. This lets your daughter know how much you delight in her and the qualities revealed in her life. It could become her first rite-of-passage ceremony as you consider later rite-of-passage celebrations throughout her life.

A Rite-of-Passage Blessing Ceremony

In May of 1999, the Lord put it on my (Doreen's) heart to create a rite of passage for our teen girls stepping into womanhood. I participated in a summit meeting in 2002 at Focus on the Family's offices in Colorado Springs, invited as one of several initiators of rite-of-passage opportunities. Amazingly, I was the only woman present. I listened as each man shared why he felt prompted to create a rite of passage for young men. Each unique plan shared a common denominator: a final ceremony with the father's blessing.

Astoundingly, the Lord had led us all to the same verse of Scripture that prompted and sealed our commitment to move forward with the passion: "He shall turn the heart of the fathers to the children, and the heart of the children to their fathers, lest I come and smite the earth with a curse" (Malachi 4:6, KJV).

Why was the verse so significant? This Scripture highlighted the loss of a father's presence in our own lives and/ or the lives of the children around us. Now, each of us had created an opportunity to seek to turn the heart of the father back to his children and the children toward their fathers.

God prompted many of us to research the Jewish community's bar or bat mitzvahs that usher their children into young adulthood in a highly celebrated fashion as described in the introduction. Their parents, prior to that pinnacle party, invested years in their journey to the coming-of-age moment.

A traditional Jewish family requires their children to memorize much of the Torah (the first five books of the Bible) by age twelve. They are taught—and it is modeled for them—the importance of faithfulness to their family and their synagogue, including attending all services together as a family. Numerous other traditions, as well as practical keys to life, are still taught in this season of their lives.

The nightly blessing by their father impacted us all. Following tradition, the father lays his hand upon their heads and speaks words of loving affirmation and hope for their futures every night! What a powerful influence on a child's life.

God saw beforehand what today's society would be like for Christians. He is the God who sees. Therefore, He knows our daughters' needs. I believe He is raising up more and more men to become better dads or "step-in-dads" to be good role models as men of integrity for our girls. Sometimes this may come in the form of grandfathers, uncles, pastors, youth leaders, older brothers, or coaches. You may know a godly man who has not been added to this list!

The power of a man is significant, though it does not lessen the power of a mother. God made male and female to complete His vision of Himself. A mom will always be her daughter's first role model. Hopefully, you and your spouse rejoice when your daughter clearly has learned a particular life lesson or begins to live out a fruit of the Spirit in her young life.

A mom is usually the one to create the birthday parties, as well as celebrations for other special moments to commemorate (such as a girl receiving Jesus into her heart or her decision to be baptized). She is the one who will whisper to God and herself, "It was worth it all," when she sees the fruit of her labor manifested in her daughter's life.

This journey through the fruit of the Spirit deserves a

celebration for both mom and daughter, who have accomplished quite a task. We hope many of the projects that reinforced a particular fruit of the Spirit made an imprint on her heart during the journey. Celebrate the completion of the journey with a rite-of-passage blessing ceremony.

You can implement your own ideas about personalizing a ceremony for your daughter, but our suggestions may get your creative juices flowing as you prepare to celebrate this rite of passage. Consider these ideas:

1. If this has been a "mommy and me study," consider having a family-and-friends celebration. If it was in a group study, proceed with your bigger audience in mind, including grandparents, friends, church family, etc.

2. Consider sending invitations with fruit as the theme.

3. Decorate your home or church. (See suggestions provided in the next section.)

4. Prepare your daughter to share the list of the fruit of the Spirit that she memorized.

5. Have her memorize the verse associated with the fruit she most enjoyed learning about to quote at the party.

6. Or she could learn the lovely vow created by Anna Minter of annaspartyworks.com, who provides group parties to learn the fruit of the Spirit together with a complementary puppet video. It reads as follows:

To make this pledge I lift my hand,
as a Daughter of the King,
I will show kindness in all the land.
My special princess life will start
By keeping the fruit of the spirit
Growing in my heart.

7. She could show off her treasure box and name each fruit of the Spirit as she pulls out her created trinkets that are her "forever reminders" of this journey.

8. You could step forward and share a memorable part of your journey with your daughter. Affirm her publicly for what a great job she did.

9. You could have her father, or another man of integrity in her life (a grandfather, uncle, etc.), publicly pray a blessing over her, emphasizing how she is growing into a young lady living out the fruit of the Spirit.

10. You or your husband could pray and place a special little crown on her head.

11. Fill out the certificate at the end of the chapter. You could frame it and present it to her at the ceremony.

12. Lead a round of applause for your daughter. Be sure she is prepared to thank each person for coming.

Princess Tea Party Book Study Launch

Introduce the book to your daughter or study group with a tea party. Fruit decorations and girls decked out like princesses create an atmosphere of excitement and joy. Centerpieces with the words of the fruit of the Spirit can help moms chat about qualities of a princess and how the coming weeks will include activities to become a true daughter of the King.

Princess Tea Party

Girls walk in dressed in beautiful clothes of bright colors. They don little crowns and color a princess coloring page. Mothers have prepared special treats that include fruit salad, fruit wand kabobs, and finger foods. The tables look lovely covered with pastel tablecloths and decorated with tea-pots. Decorations of paper fruits and butterflies reflect a garden scene.

Girls play games and hold a princess dance to praise music and a princess parade. A princess story focuses on all the things a princess can do. The girls' smiles and laughter fill the room. Cameras snap to capture memories of the festive atmosphere.

The speaker wears a crown and pretty dress too. She says, "Welcome to all our princesses. Do you want to be a real princess in God's kingdom? That means becoming a royal daughter, one who develops wonderful fruits of faithfulness, peace, joy, goodness, gentleness, kindness, patience, and love. Raise your hands to show you want to be a princess." The speaker chats about fruitful actions and how to be a princess-in-action.

Girls giggle as they make princess creations, and mothers smile as they look at their beautiful, happy daughters. It's always a delight to see our daughters smile and begin a journey that brings them closer to God and develop virtues.

Continuing the Journey

What's next? That's the question most often asked as we come to the end of a rite-of-passage ceremony.

The following suggestions and recommendations provide support as you continue the journey and guide your daughter into becoming a true princess and help her continue to embrace her identity as a daughter of the King.

1. Consider returning to the activities in this book once a week. Choose activities you didn't try before, or do a favorite one to reinforce the fruit of the Spirit. This may equip you with different activities for more than a year!

2. A complementary daily resource for your little girl is *The One Year My Princess Devotions*, preschool edition, authored by Karen Whiting. Find free related resources at karenwhiting.com/freedownloads.

3. As you begin to discover your daughter's gifts and talents, seek resources that will assist her development (such as piano lessons, art classes, ice-skating sessions, or even karate training for self-defense).

4. Strengthen her princess social skills by enrolling her in a children's camp. Or go camping together as a family. You'll have fun while she learns about nature, discovers how to make new friends, and learns to appreciate family time. Other options might include sports camp, day camp, or summer camp based on her special interests.

5. Throw an annual tea party for your princess and her friends. It's a great way to teach proper manners. Each year, add age-appropriate etiquette tips. Ideas can be accessed at courteousandcool.com. Or use the book *365 Manners Kids Should Know* by Sheryl Eberly.

6. American Heritage Girls, established in 1995, is a Christian-based scouting organization for girls ages five to eighteen. Its purpose is to embrace Christian values, and the organization encourages family involvement to build and develop character and social and leadership skills in our girls. Visit this group at americanheritagegirls.org.

7. *Raising a Modern-Day Princess*, published by Focus on the Family/Tyndale, addresses parents and mentors of girls ages twelve to eighteen. It presents the value and purpose of providing a biblically based rite of passage for girls stepping into womanhood. Related resources available include the *Becoming a Modern Day Princess Leader's Guide* and *Becoming a Modern-Day Princess Journal* at moderndayprincess.net.

8. Her sexual purity will be an important topic in her future. You'll find recommended books at focusonthefamily.com/lifechallenges/love-and-sex. Another excellent resource is available at familylife.com/Passport2Purity.

9. MOPS (Mothers of Preschoolers), originally established for mothers of young children, expanded their ministry

to encourage and reenergize moms through groups in local neighborhoods. Visit mops.org.

10. Moms in Prayer International is an organization that unites mothers around the world to meet and pray for the lives of their children in school. Join or start a group in your school or church by visiting momsinprayer.org.

11. Take care of yourself. Leadinghearts.com offers resources and a magazine that includes a column by Karen Whiting that equips Christian women to be leaders and live worthy lives.

12. Here are some books recommended especially for dads:

- *The Dads & Daughters Togetherness Guide* by Joe Kelly. Includes fifty-four fun activities to help build a great relationship.
- *10 Things Great Dads Do: Strategies for Raising Great Kids* by Rick Johnson.

Fruitful Activities

Celebration Ideas

Launch the fruit of the Spirit activities for girls with a tea party, and celebrate the completion with a blessing ceremony and party.

Decorations

Let girls fill baskets or crystal bowls with colorful fruit. Decorate the room with plants and colorful pails holding gardening tools. Wrap purple tulle around each chair back and tie in a bow.

Foods

Fruit salad, fruit punch, and fruit kabobs add to the theme. Add a star-cut piece of fruit at the end to make a starry wand. Serve fruit breads and muffins, such as banana, apple, or strawberry. Make a cake in the shape of a fruit or a cornucopia filled with fruit.

Games

- Make pairs of cards with pictures of fruits and crowns for a game of Concentration. On matching cards, write the words from Galatians 5:22-23, the fruit of the Spirit. You can print out enough sets on card stock for each girl to take a set home. Or use index cards cut in half combined with fruit, crowns, and heart stickers for girls to make cards.

- *Pin the Jewels on the Crown.* Make a large crown to hang on a wall at a girl's shoulder height. Cut out paper in big jewel shapes and write a fruit of the Spirit on each one (such as joy, peace, kindness, etc.). Play the game as you would play Pin the Tail on the Donkey.

- *Fruit of the Spirit Switch.* Give every girl a paper with a fruit on it. Have all but one of the girls sit in a circle on chairs. The lone girl stands in the circle and calls out, "Everyone with the fruit of (fill in the blank), switch." The girls with that fruit should jump up and find a new seat while the girl in the middle scrambles to grab a seat. The one left without a seat is the new "it."

- *Pass the Fruit Ball.* On a beach ball, write names of the fruit of the Spirit. Draw fruit shapes around the words. Toss the ball. The princess who catches it names one type of fruit; she should also say one way to show that fruit. Then she tosses the ball for another princess to catch.

Crafts

- Slice apples and oranges in half to let girls make apple prints. Cut some apples crosswise to reveal how the seeds form a star inside the apple.

- Have a fruit hunt for paper or real fruit. Ask girls to bring baskets, or pass out paper bags to collect the fruits.

- Use the acrostic from the book to make bookmarks. Punch a hole in the top and add a yarn or ribbon tassel.

- String O-shaped fruit cereal on elastic thread to make bracelets or necklaces. Girls can munch on the leftover cereal.

- Make princess glitter gel: mix with two teaspoons nonpetroleum jelly (found in health food stores) with two and a half tablespoons aloe vera gel. Sprinkle in fine cosmetic body glitter a little at a time and test to see if there's enough glitter. If not, add more. If there's too much, add more gel.

- *Fruit of the Spirit Booklets.* Layer and fold three sheets of half-page pieces of colored paper or card stock to form booklets. Provide crown stickers for the cover and write "Princess _____ (fill in girl's name)."

Inside the cover add the date started. Use the next nine pages to list each of the fruits of the Spirit (love, joy, patience, etc.) and add pictures of fruits. Inside the back cover save room for the girl's photo and the date she worked on all the fruits.

- *Fruit of the Spirit Bookmarks.* Cut card stock into two-by-seven-inch strips. Let the girls add fruit stickers. Make stickers with the fruit of the Spirit by printing them on clear address labels. Let girls add the labels to their bookmarks. Option: Older girls can print the words.

Dad and Daughter Activities

Love Letters

Write your daughter a "love letter" at least once a year and include a prayer for blessings from God for the coming year.

Frame and Hang the Blessing Certificate

Use a carpenter's level to hang a picture and chat about the need to place a picture correctly. The level's bubbles will balance when the line is straight. Point out that we all need balance in life.

Capture the Memories

The years pass too quickly and become mere memories. Save and savor the moments with photos and words in a scrapbook or online journal.

Use a journal to record your daughter's progress in developing the fruit of the Spirit. Snap photos and create a scrapbook of your daughter exhibiting the qualities we have studied.

· THIS ROYAL ·

Certificate

~ CERTIFIES THAT ~

HAS BECOME A

True Princess

—— INDEED ——

SHE HAS COMPLETED HER

Fruit of the Spirit Journey

True Princess

SIGNED: DATED:

Dad's Toolbox

A carpenter's level is referred to as a *plumb* or *spirit level* according to both the Merriam-Webster dictionary and TheFree Dictionary.com. *Plumb* means "in perfect alignment." A spirit level uses an air bubble in a tube filled with alcohol. When the bubble is centered inside the level, it confirms perfect balance. A complete toolbox will contain a spirit level. For a man seeking to make his project one of perfection, it's a defining moment when his level confirms he has fulfilled his goal.

Blessings are like a level. They are words spoken, or written, to confirm that someone has looked into a person's life and deemed it to be in balance. Webster's definition of *balance* is "a condition in which different elements are equal or in the correct proportions." As a father, is that the greatest desire of your heart—to see that your daughter's character traits, gifts, and abilities are in balance? This is possible as you wisely use the tools in your Dad's Toolbox according to her needs and faithfully impart your words of blessing. You will be working to keep all things in alignment in her life through prayer and example.

As you use your level to evaluate your own life, as well as your daughter's, may you see that your lives stand upright before God and those around you.

Mommy, I wish you were my age so
you can be my daughter.

MARLEY, age 5, littlehoots.com

Discussion Guide

WE (DOREEN AND KAREN) have greatly loved being mothers and raising daughters. Through the years we have known the joy of seeing our daughters make good choices and begin to follow God's plan for their lives. We've also dealt with difficulties when they made poor choices. We are both thankful our daughters grew into wonderful women whose lives most often show the fruit of the Spirit. We pray that you, too, will know the joy of raising a daughter of the King, a true Modern-Day Princess.

Read Galatians 5:22-23, and reflect on the fruit of the Holy Spirit. Also read Proverbs 31:10-31, and notice how this woman's actions reveal those fruits. Let those passages be your guiding Scriptures as you raise your daughter.

We used two acrostics with the word *princess* as guides for the mother's role and the desired daughter's attributes that will produce the fruit. Review the chart and discuss the mother's role and the desired outcomes.

Mother's actions	Princess attributes	Resulting fruit
P-erceive	**P**-rayerful	*Faithfulness*
R-efine	**R**-espectful	*Peace*
I-nspire	**I**-nspired	*Joy*
N-urture	**N**-oble	*Goodness*
C-ultivate	**C**-ompassionate	*Gentleness*
E-ncourage	**E**-ncourager	*Kindness*
S-how Her	**S**-elf-controlled	*Patience and self-control*
S-erve	**S**-ervant	*Love*

Introduction

1. What special dreams do you have for your daughter or daughters?

2. What does it mean to be a daughter of the King? What does this look like in your own journey?

3. Have you ever been part of a rite-of-passage ceremony? Describe it. Why was it meaningful?

4. Who was an influential mentor in your life? What was special about your relationship?

5. Why is gardening an appropriate metaphor for the process of raising a daughter?

CHAPTER ONE: *Guiding and Growing a Daughter of the King*

1. Describe a father's role in a daughter's life. How is it different from a mother's role?

2. Do you have a teachable spirit? Does your daughter show a teachable spirit? Why is this important when it comes to being a daughter of the King?

3. What is your daughter's personality profile? What is yours?

4. How do your personalities complement each other or potentially create a challenge?

CHAPTER TWO: *The Fruit of Faithfulness in Your Princess's Life*

1. What is the world's view of a princess today? How is that different from being a daughter of the King, a true princess?

2. How do you pray with your princess? How do you expect prayer to produce faithfulness?

3. Why is it important to be a perceiving mother? What does that look like in your own relationship with your daughter?

4. Did you create a treasure box with your daughter? What items did you put into it? What did they represent to you and to her?

5. How did you use the prayer ABCs? How do you plan to use them in the future?

CHAPTER THREE: *The Fruit of Peace in Your Princess's Life*

1. What is your greatest challenge in modeling respectful behavior?

2. What are the biggest problems that prompt whining and fighting in your daughter?

3. What tips from the chapter will you use to bring more peace?

4. Did you create a family identity? If so, share its significance and the importance of this activity.

5. When have you seen your daughter make progress in being obedient and respectful?

CHAPTER FOUR: *The Fruit of Joy in Your Princess's Life*

1. What brings you pleasure and happiness?

2. When have you felt deep joy?

3. What inspires your daughter's joy?

4. What prompts your daughter's creativity?

5. How will you help your daughter experience joy this week?

CHAPTER FIVE: *The Fruit of Goodness in Your Princess's Life*

1. How is Proverbs 31 a guide for you to become a noble woman?

2. What qualities do you want to see revealed in yourself and your daughter?

3. What act of goodness can you and your daughter do together and then share with others this week?

4. Did you work on starting a "Goodness Album"? Share what you included in it.

CHAPTER SIX: *The Fruit of Gentleness in Your Princess's Life*

1. What is your definition of gentleness? How does it differ from goodness?

2. Share a story about when someone has shown compassion to you. What did it mean to you?

3. Do you remember a time when your daughter was gentle or compassionate?

4. What are some creative ways you are helping your daughter develop compassion?

CHAPTER SEVEN: *The Fruit of Kindness in Your Princess's Life*

1. What encourages you as a mother?

2. How do you intentionally encourage your daughter?

3. In what areas does your daughter need encouragement?

4. When have you seen your daughter being kind?

CHAPTER EIGHT: *The Fruit of Patience and Self-Control*

1. Why are both patience and self-control difficult for us in today's culture?

2. How do you react when you are angry?

3. How do you respond to your daughter's anger?

4. What do you do to help your daughter learn patience and self-control?

CHAPTER NINE: *The Fruit of Love in Your Princess's Life*

1. What has been a memorable act of love that you have experienced?

2. Who immediately comes to mind when you hear the words "a faithful servant"?

3. How do you encourage your daughter to be a loving servant?

4. What deeds of service does your daughter enjoy doing?

CHAPTER TEN: *Continuing the Journey as a Daughter of the King*

1. How will you commemorate the journey of raising your daughter and nurturing fruits of the Spirit?

2. How do you capture memories of watching your daughter grow and exhibit fruits of the Spirit? Why is it important to do so?

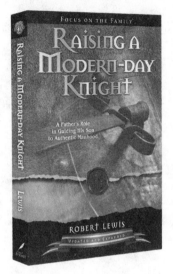

Meet the rest of the family

**Expert advice on parenting and marriage . . .
spiritual growth . . . powerful personal stories . . .**

Focus on the Family's collection of inspiring, practical resources can help your family grow closer to God—and each other—than ever before. Whichever format you need—video, audio, book, or e-book—we have something for you. Discover how to help your family thrive with books, DVDs, and more at **FocusOnTheFamily.com/resources.**